Mapping Inner Space

Learning and Teaching Visual Mapping

Nancy Margulies

with Nusa Maal

Materials provided by:
The Florida Inclusion Network
UCF/Daytona Beach
386-274-0360
Toll Free: 1-877-346-8233
The Florida Inclusion Network is funded by
The Florida Department of Education, Bureau of
Exceptional Education and Student Services.

Zephyr Press

Chicago

Mapping Inner Space
Learning and Teaching Visual Mapping

Grades K–12 and adult

© 2002 Zephyr Press
Printed in the United States of America

ISBN: 1-56976-138-8

Editing: Melanie Mallon
Design & Production: Dan Miedaner
Cover: Nancy Margulies
Illustrations: Nancy Margulies and Nusa Maal

Mind Maps are the registered trademark of the Buzan Organization, used here with enthusiastic permission.

Published by Zephyr Press
An imprint of Chicago Review Press, Incorpated
814 North Franklin Street
Chicago, Illinois 60610
(800)232-2187
www.zephyrpress.com

Library of Congress Cataloging-in-Publication Data

Margulies, Nancy, 1947-
    Mapping inner space : learning and teaching visual mapping / Nancy Margulies with
    Nusa Maal.—2nd ed.
        p. cm.
    Includes bibliographical references and index.
    ISBN 1-56976-138-8
        1. Visual learning. 2. Thought and thinking. I. Maal, Nusa. II. Title.

LB1067.5 .M37 2001
153.1'52—dc21   2001035982

"This marvelous book will be of tremendous help to all of us who are learning to think systemically."
—Fritjof Capra
author of *The Web of Life*

"Here is a book and technique as profound as it is practical. The author is the maestra of Mind Mapping and the reader who follows her powerful processes will awaken to new life and new being."
—Jean Houston
author of *Jump Time* and *Mythic Life*

"Visual mapping is a superb tool both for communication and for personal reflection. Read this wonderful book and learn how to use it in your own work."
—Parker J. Palmer
author of *Let Your Life Speak* and *The Courage to Teach*

"Nancy's maps captivate and catapult one into a world of thinking in pictures."
—Judy Bekker
Director, Facilitator, Renaissance Business Associates, Cape Town, South Africa

"Her work takes Mind Mapping to higher levels of conceptualization by adding powerful visual mnemonics, linking ideas and boosting memory for later recall."
—Barbara Given, Ph.D.
Director, Adolescent Learning Research Center, Krasnow Institute for Advanced Study, George Mason University, Fairfax, Virginia

"Mapping Inner Space is a priceless tool . . . Mapping is of particular value for groups from diverse cultural and linguistic backgrounds and varied levels of schooling. By complementing the written word with visual communication it taps on multiple senses of intelligence, facilitating intercultural dialogues."
—Gabriela Melano, M.Ed.
Consulting Services in Conflict Resolution and Decision Making Processes, Systems Thinking, Cross-cultural and Group Graphics Expertise

Acknowledgments

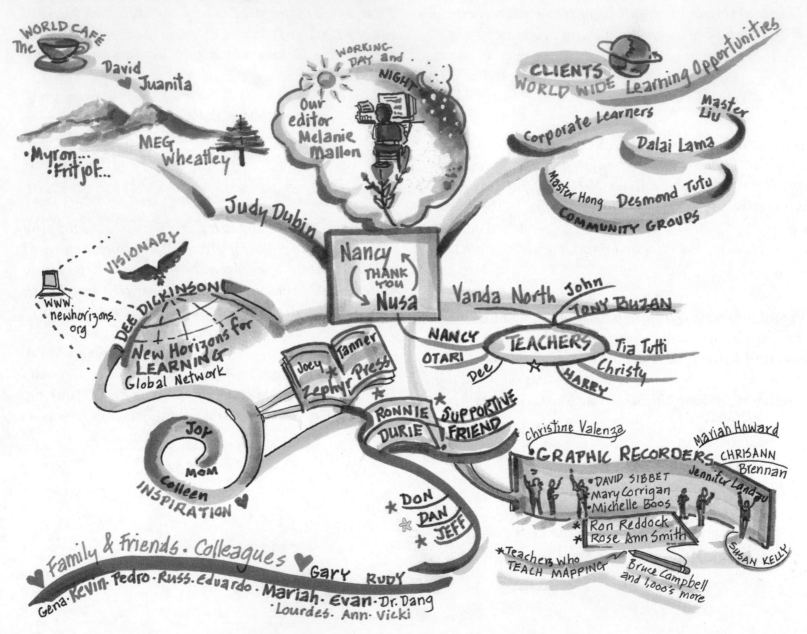

Mapping Inner Space ©2002 www.zephyrpress.com

About This Book

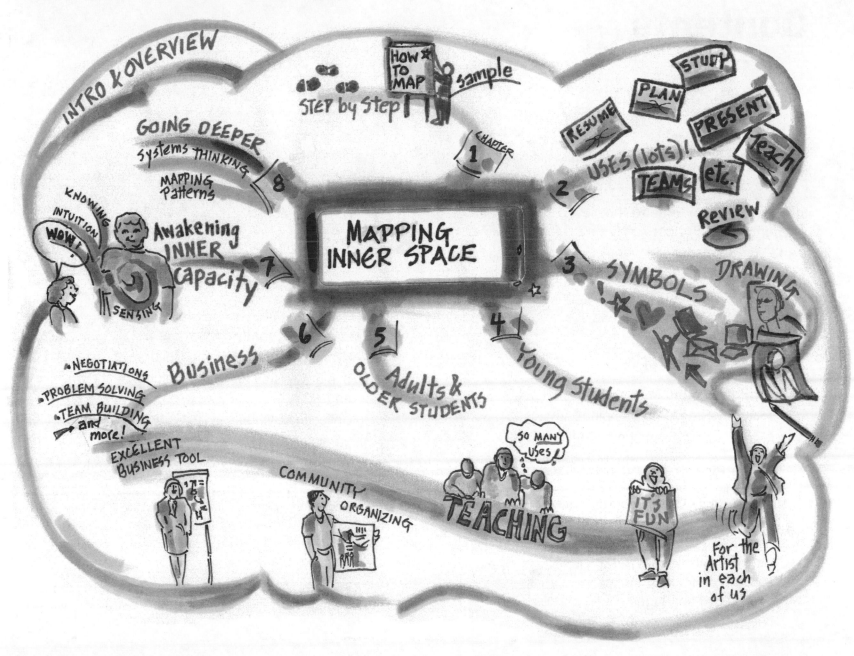

Contents

Foreword

Every so often, one of Nancy's mindscapes falls off my bookcase and into my awareness. I always pick up the booklet and find myself instantly back in time, in the seminar represented in her drawings. Time disappears, memory flourishes. Ideas that I'd forgotten leap off the page. Moments of learning or tension or laughter in the group come vividly to mind. The range of faces and feelings comes back into focus.

Nancy drew these memorable images at seminars on self-organizing systems we cofacilitated at Sundance, Utah, for several years. While some of us spoke, and 60 to 80 organizational leaders listened, Nancy captured our ideas, comments, and significant learnings. We couldn't have dealt well with the richness, the challenge, and the wonder of the concepts we were exploring in new science without these mindscapes. As they went up on large wall charts, we saw the individual ideas and, more important, their inter-relationships. We could literally see what we were trying to understand—the systemic nature of life.

I can't imagine learning how to think systemically without some sort of visual imagery, without seeing the system swim on the page, flowing onto the next page. I can't imagine remembering the complexity of concepts without seeing them up on a large chart and then connected effortlessly to other ideas. Only some of us are visual learners, yet everyone learns more when ideas take shape in the clear and creative ways that Nancy and Nusa describe in these pages.

And once the words and shapes are on the page, they are there for us to remember. We actually remember what we've thought about and what we've learned. And we remember whom we learned it with, and what it felt like to be there with them.

One more thing I've learned from Nancy. We are all creative. Far too many of us have forgotten that, but now we have this book. As you read it, you will feel Nancy and Nusa encouraging you, helping you remember that we are all capable of so much more than we think. This book is a gift in many ways: It gives us processes for real learning. It details techniques that lead to true problem solving. It teaches methods that bring us together in better relationships and that make us smarter. But the richest gift of this book is that it brings us back to ourselves. We are all creative.

—Margaret J. Wheatley
author of *Leadership and the New Science*
and coauthor of *A Simpler Way*

Preface

My life has been greatly affected as a result of practicing mapping and developing my own style of visual recording. As I became more comfortable with drawing and developed an ability to listen carefully to key ideas, I found that my skill as a learner improved. I can now record ideas from almost any field and have been able to take part in fascinating conferences and meetings all over the world. My favorites include mapping with Maori tribes in New Zealand as we developed strategies for their land-claim presentations, recording a day-long strategic planning meeting for President Clinton and the cabinet, and mapping while the Dalai Lama met with world leaders from various fields of study.

Beyond these exciting events is something deeper. I now can see patterns, relationships, and systems with an overview that I never had before. By far the greatest benefit for me is that visual mapping has developed my thinking skills.

For this second edition of *Mapping Inner Space,* I invited Nusa Maal to lend her insights and skill to the book. Ten years ago, we discovered our common interests and a deep sense of shared purpose. Nusa worked extensively with one of the developers of Mind Mapping, Tony Buzan. She then branched off to develop her own creative approaches to visual mapping, drawing, and awakening deeper understanding through accessing multisensory intelligence. We both contributed to this edition, but decided to use the word "I" to refer to either one of us in most cases.

Our hope is that *Mapping Inner Space* will contribute to a future in which all children experience the joy of visual mapping as a method of self-expression and note taking. Through our explorations in this field, we've discovered depths of inner and group intelligence that visual mapping can awaken and set in motion in people of all ages. With this book we invite you to tap your own capacities as creative, artistic explorers of the amazing world around us, and the profound uncharted worlds within.

—**Nancy Margulies**
2001

Introduction

Welcome to the New Mapping Inner Space

Mind Mapping is an easy-to-learn, straightforward system for generating and organizing any ideas. Using a central image, key words, colors, codes, and symbols, the process is both fun and fast. For many of us, the traditional style of writing ideas in a linear fashion, using one color on lined paper, is a deeply ingrained habit. Retraining the brain to draw ideas radiating from a central image takes practice and patience. However, after you have the basics of Mind Mapping down, the obvious benefits will lead you to use this technique any time you want to put ideas on paper. This book presents a variety of maps, beginning with standardized Mind Maps and then numerous free-form variations, called *Visual Maps* or *Mindscapes*. Once you learn to let your ideas and associations flow freely, you will no doubt create your own maps of previously unexplored territories.

Mapping Is for Everyone

More than ten years ago, when *Mapping Inner Space* was first published, a few teachers were using this creative technique and teaching it to their students. Today mapping is used widely in schools, universities, and the corporate world as well. The process has evolved to include many varieties of visual mapping and has spawned entirely new career fields called *graphic* (or *visual*) *recording* and *graphic facilitation*.

The invitation to be creative while recording ideas, to use color and visual symbols along with words and phrases, is appealing to most students and many adult learners as well. This book explores a variety of mapping styles and also takes a fresh look at the process of learning. Learning isn't just for kids anymore! Corporate executives, community organizers, leaders in all walks of life have come to recognize and value lifelong learning. That is why the second edition of *Mapping Inner Space* is not only for teachers and their students; it is equally important for parents, business people, retired citizens—anyone who wants to add challenge and creativity to his or her life.

Visual Maps Are Natural

Visual note taking is nothing new. You can see it in primitive cave paintings, the hieroglyphics of ancient Egypt, and the notes and sketches of such great thinkers as Leonardo da Vinci and Michelangelo. Left to their own devices, most children and many adults sketch and doodle while listening to new ideas.

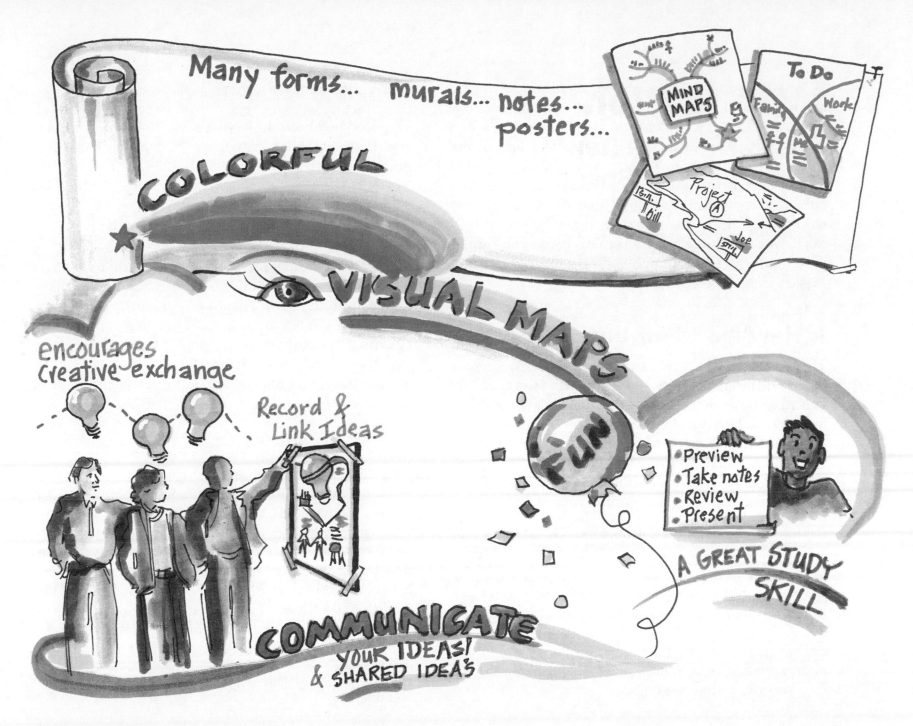

Before we establish language, we visualize pictures in our minds and link them to concepts. Throughout our lives the inner knowing that we sometimes call *intuition* appears as an image or sensation long before we can articulate it in words. Unfortunately, we often block the creative channels by training children to write only words, monochromatically, on lined paper. Now that many educators are aware of the value of nurturing thinking skills and creativity, we can employ systems like visual mapping that don't restrict, but rather promote, creative thinking.

A New World for Learners

The skills that we must nurture and develop today are utterly different from those we needed in the past. Not long ago, the primary goal of education was preparation for work. Today education is best described as a lifelong process that takes place everywhere: school, the workplace, home, and community. We now recognize that learners have vastly different styles for taking in information and making meaning from it.

In this age of computers, people don't need to become storehouses for facts and dates. The challenge is for us to do what computers can't—develop our humanity, creativity, intuition, unique perspectives, and human ingenuity. Each of us must be able to work well individually and with others in mutually supportive exchanges. Mapping enables us to express our understanding as we take in and transform information into knowledge and wisdom.

One of the most reassuring aspects of the challenge to educators is that we already have a wealth of powerful knowledge about how to teach in dynamic and multisensory styles that bring out the best in each individual learner.

Brain-Friendly Learning for All Ages

One of the primary reasons that we are now better equipped to become lifelong learners is that we have increasing amounts of information about the workings of the human brain. Although we can't always be certain how best to translate brain research into teaching techniques, we can look to neuroscience to reinforce our own observations, challenge our assumptions, and raise important questions.

We now understand that the notion of right and left hemispheres each handling specific tasks is far too simple to explain the workings of our brains. However, it is useful to be aware that one of our processing styles is global and dominates when we are engaged in nonverbal activities, such as relaxing while listening to music, drawing, and using our imagination. When we focus our thoughts via language, solve math problems, and process data in a linear, sequential manner, a different processing style is dominant. Our traditional methods of recording ideas encourage us to move from one idea to the next in a sequential, concrete fashion. Note taking of this sort can limit our ability to see the big picture, patterns, and connections among the ideas we're recording. When mapping, we are

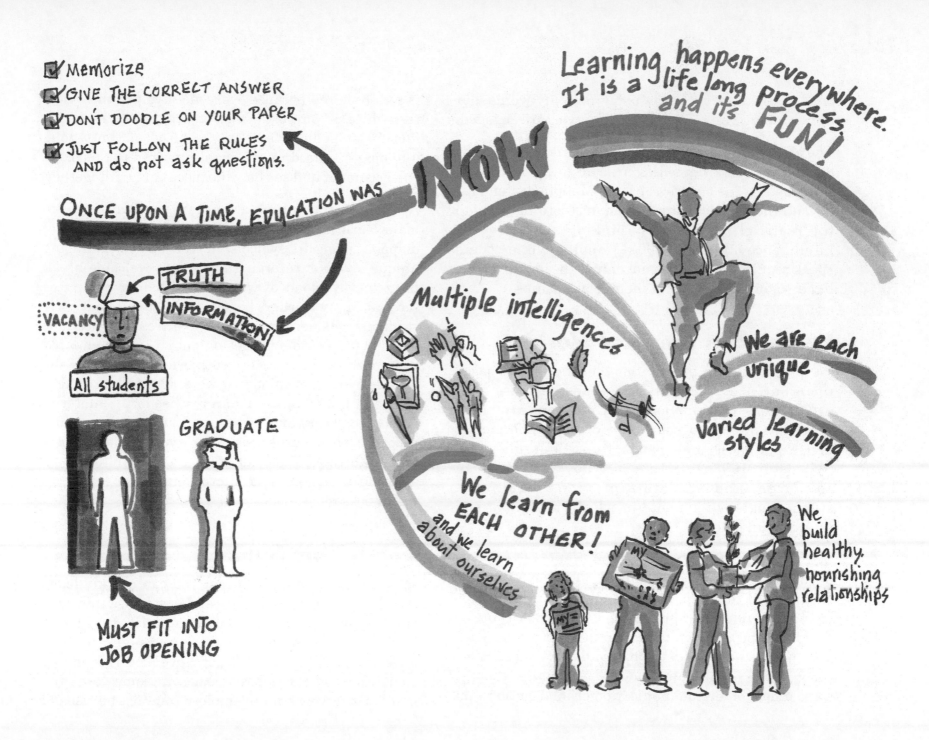

- ☑ Memorize
- ☑ GIVE THE CORRECT ANSWER
- ☑ DON'T DOODLE ON YOUR PAPER
- ☑ JUST FOLLOW THE RULES AND do not ask questions.

ONCE UPON A TIME, EDUCATION WAS

Now

Learning happens everywhere. It is a life long process and its **FUN!**

TRUTH
INFORMATION

VACANCY

All students

GRADUATE

MUST FIT INTO JOB OPENING

Multiple intelligences

We are each unique

Varied learning styles

We learn from EACH OTHER! and we learn about ourselves

We build healthy nourishing relationships

MY

challenged to record ideas using not only words, but also symbols. Thus both processing styles are engaged.

The ability to put thoughts into images as well as words enhances thinking skills and actually improves intelligence. The benefits of Mind Mapping extend far beyond the practical application of recording ideas to the realm of higher-order thinking and increased intelligence (Wenger 1990). Mapping while others speak requires us to listen not only to the flow of words, but also for key ideas and their relationships.

Mapping in the Real World

We all organize the information that comes to us based upon our past experiences, values, purpose, and expectations. Our emotional responses and attention, which link directly to memory, are drawn to information and experiences that matter to us (Margulies and Sylwester 1998a). If this is true, then how can employers and educators provide meaningful, stimulating environments in which motivation and interest run high?

Mapping a project or subject to be studied is one way of introducing the whole and engaging our feelings. Elements of the map, details added, and connections drawn provide the parts of the project in context. Further, if people map their own understanding, each has an opportunity to develop, record, and share unique perspectives on the same topic. In workplaces there is a great deal of miscommunication or information that is never shared because everyone involved may view the "whole" or purpose of a given project differently. In fact, most people have only a piece of the whole. Mapping a shared image enables everyone to look at one document and see how the pieces may fit together.

Another aspect of stimulating learners of any age is to make learning more fun and rewarding. The process of mapping, using art, symbols, and color, and encouraging unique styles of recording ideas, is a welcome break from the overload of words on paper or computer screens. Many teachers have reported to me that their students consider mapping to be a treat. Notice how engaging the student maps on page 73 are compared to an outline. Further, the teacher feels as if he or she can look into the minds of the students and take a glance at how they are making sense of the material presented. Every map is different, just as the internal process of each learner is unique. Every Mind Map is a view into the unique territory created by our own amazing brains—into the multifaceted inner space that we all possess.

About This Book

This book is organized so that you can quickly learn the Mind Mapping technique and how to use it in your home, business, school, and community. I will also introduce a variety of other styles of visual recording. Most pages of text in this book have a corresponding visual map on the opposite page. In some cases the map will serve as an example of one of the uses of

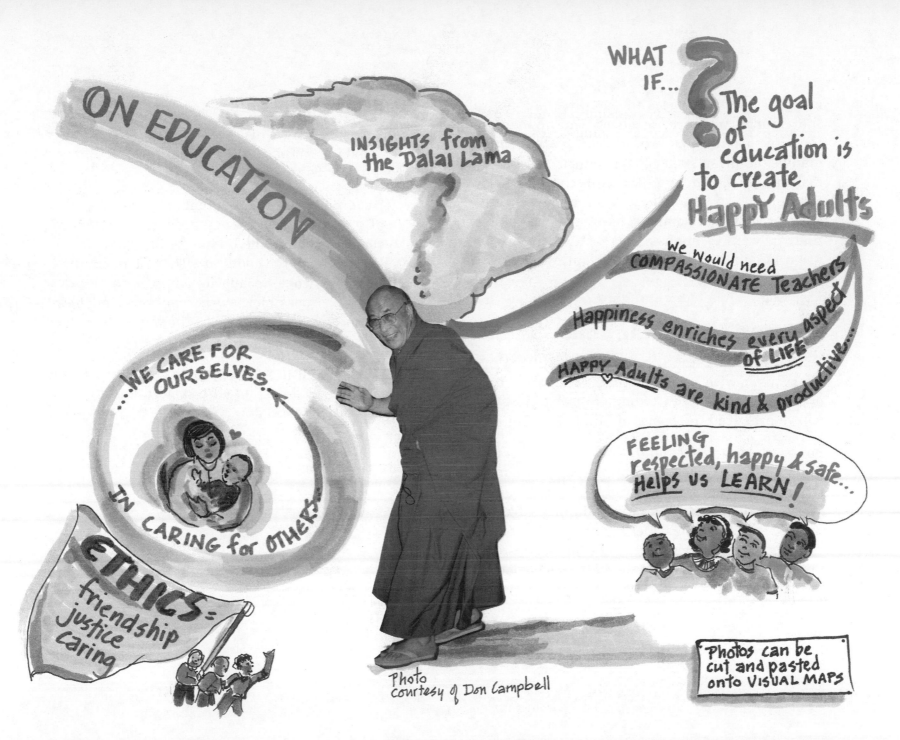

ON EDUCATION

INSIGHTS from the Dalai Lama

WHAT IF... ?

The goal of education is to create Happy Adults

we would need COMPASSIONATE Teachers

Happiness enriches every aspect of LIFE

HAPPY Adults are kind & productive...

...WE CARE FOR OURSELVES...

IN CARING for OTHERS...

ETHICS = friendship justice caring

FEELING respected, happy & safe... Helps us LEARN!

Photos can be cut and pasted onto VISUAL MAPS

Photo courtesy of Don Campbell

mapping; in other cases the map will loosely reflect the information presented on the opposite page. Usually, visual maps are in color. We have included many examples of color maps, but in some cases, the maps are black and white. Feel free to photocopy any of the maps as handouts or to create overheads. You can add color to the maps by highlighting the elements that you want to emphasize or remember. You can also use colored felt-tip pens to add your own ideas to the maps in this book.

Beyond Mind Mapping

Once you understand and practice Mind Mapping, experiment with any style that works for you. Other approaches to visual recording are easy to develop after you've practiced the basics of Mind Mapping.

For teachers, parents, and other instructors, the best approach is to become comfortable with mapping through practice, then introduce it to others. After you've begun with basic Mind Mapping, feel free to develop and share new ideas, forms, and applications. Think of mapping as a flexible, evolving system with unlimited potential—like the vast inner space of the human mind itself.

Infinite Possibilities

Norman Cousins, in his excellent book on the power of the mind in healing entitled *Head First: The Biology of Hope,* describes the brain:

> Not even the universe, with its countless billions of galaxies, represents greater wonder or complexity than the human brain. The human brain is a mirror to infinity. There is no limit to its range, scope, or capacity for creative growth. It makes possible new perceptions and new perspectives, just as it clears the way for brighter prospects in human affairs. (Cousins 1989, 71)

You are invited to follow Norman Cousins's insights and plunge head-first into the exploration of your own infinite inner space.

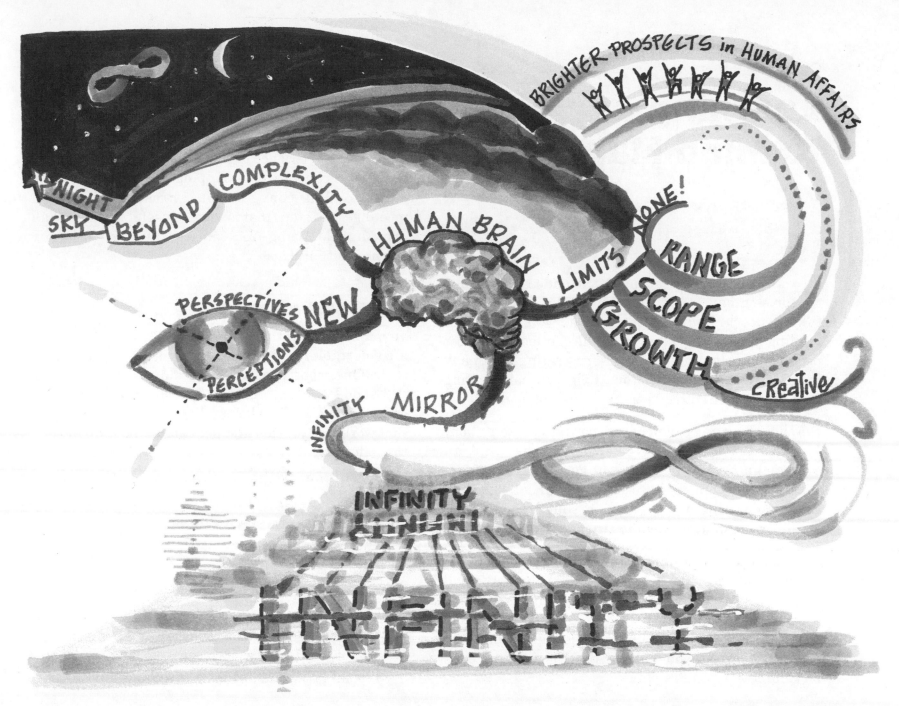

NIGHT SKY · BEYOND · COMPLEXITY

HUMAN BRAIN

BRIGHTER PROSPECTS in HUMAN AFFAIRS

NEW PERSPECTIVES · PERCEPTIONS

LIMITS · NONE!

RANGE · SCOPE · GROWTH · Creative

INFINITY MIRROR

INFINITY

INFINITY

Chapter 1

Learning to Mind Map

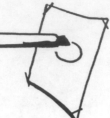

Think about the last time you attended a workshop or seminar. Do you remember the experience of taking notes? More important, do you remember reading your notes later to recall the lecture? Most people report that note taking is frustrating, and many have so much trouble reading their own handwriting that they never bother to refer to the notes again.

How about writing a paper or preparing a presentation? If the mere thought gives you shivers and an overwhelming urge to clean your garage, then you are not alone. Mapping is a process that will enable you to enjoy generating and organizing your thoughts and skillfully presenting them to others.

Mind Mapping is a quick way to take notes that are easy to read and seem to organize themselves. As you'll see, when Mind Mapping, your thoughts become distilled into essential key words. You can present many concepts in a single meaning-rich symbol. Once you get the hang of it, you will find that getting started is no trouble—it's child's play.

Step-by-Step Mind Mapping

The easiest way to begin mapping is to record your *own* thoughts and generate new ideas in the process. This form of individual brainstorming will give you an immediate experience of the power of Mind Mapping. Later, you can practice mapping ideas presented by others during conversations, presentations, and meetings. The steps that follow are useful for more than just Mind Mapping. You can use these steps in any learning situation.

Step One: Prepare

To map your own thoughts, set aside 30 minutes, find a comfortable, well-lit place to work, and think of a topic. Questions that are important to you, such as "What do I want in a relationship?" or "How can I build on my strengths?" make excellent topics. Other topics that work well for this first personal Mind Map include the following:

- plans for the day (week, month, quarter, etc.)
- goals for the year (or the next five, ten, twenty years)
- memories of a specific event
- strategies for a new project
- interests and hobbies
- the highlights of a book you recently read
- your skills and talents and those you want to develop
- your *ideal* future
- points you want to discuss in a phone conversation

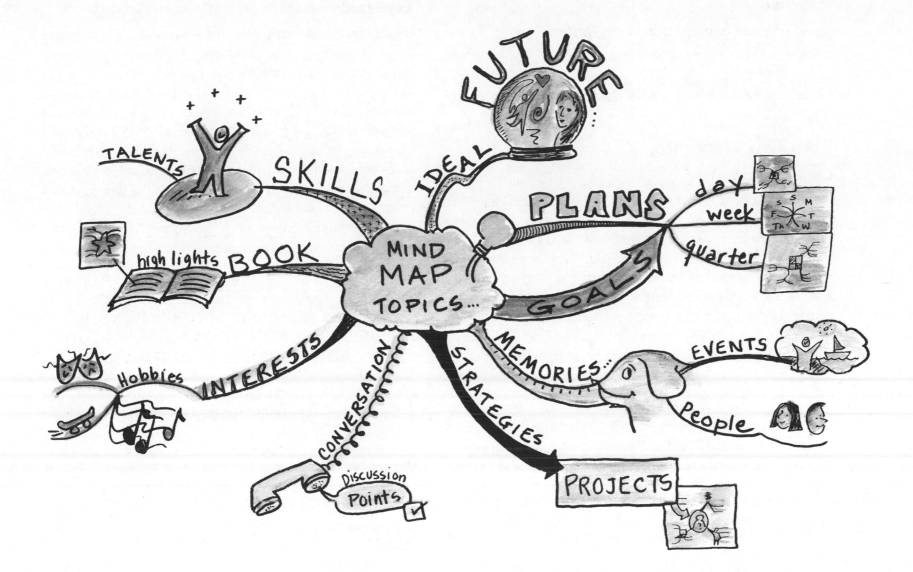

FUTURE

TALENTS SKILLS IDEAL

PLANS day week quarter

high lights BOOK

MIND MAP TOPICS...

GOALS

MEMORIES...

EVENTS

Hobbies INTERESTS

CONVERSATION

STRATEGIES

People

DISCUSSION Points

PROJECTS

Materials

- ✔ unlined paper, 11" x 17" or larger
- ✔ medium felt-tip markers or pens in a variety of colors
- ✔ several broad-tip pastel markers for highlighting

Step Two: Generate

Central Image

Begin by drawing a picture or symbol that represents your topic. Draw the image in the center of the paper and keep it fairly small so you have plenty of room left for the ideas you will be recording. (Notice the size of the central image in the maps in this book.) If you draw a symbol and then wonder if you will be able to remember what it represents, write a word or two next to the picture. If you are absolutely stuck and can't think of an image for your topic, just draw a colorful cloud or another shape and a few words. Later you can return to the center and fill out the image.

From this central image, draw branching lines that radiate out. Notice how the lines resemble the branches or roots of a tree as they expand at the base and taper toward the ends. You can color in the branches for emphasis or to show a connection between related ideas by making those branches the same color.

Key Words

Use key words in your mapping: Key words are meaning-rich words that may lead to many other associations. The words that you select will be ones that convey the most information. Obviously, words such as "of, the, it," and "an" are not key words (unless you are mapping a plot for "The Day IT Ate Cleveland"). Choose *one* word for each branch of your map instead of several words or phrases. Learning to select just one key word will help you develop the habit of paring down your notes to the truly essential elements. You'll also learn to listen for key points and rapidly grasp the essence of a presentation, conversation, or meeting.

This one-word system will enable you to associate freely and add branches. For example, the word MARKETING might lead you to think of DIRECT, INDIRECT, TELEPHONE, CUSTOMERS, and so forth. If you had written DIRECT MAIL MARKETING as a phrase, you might not have arrived at an insight such as "phone existing customers." Imagine how useful this process of free association is for students as well as business people.

Print: Have you ever noticed that sometimes your hastily dashed-off notes are mysteriously replaced with a totally illegible scrawl? You are not alone. Printing the words is a quick cure for the hard-to-read-notes phenomenon. Printed words may take a bit longer, but they are not only easier to read, they are more memorable as well.

Mind Mapping Basics

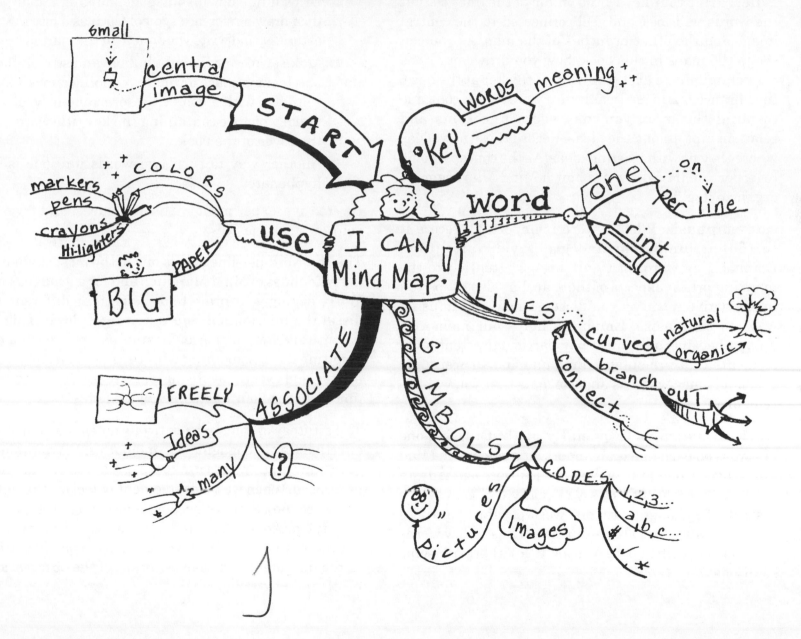

Lines: Print your key words on top of the lines so that the words will look and feel connected to the central image and the other branches of the map. As you can see in the maps in this book, how you draw your lines can communicate a lot. Draw them thicker at the base, then branch out in an organic direction. As you continue to build the map, you may see connections and relationships among the ideas. Record these new ideas where they fit with existing ideas. As the concepts come together you'll begin to see how a Mind Map seems to organize itself.

Add emphasis: When a word is important, record it so that it jumps out and grabs your attention. Emphasizing words not only brings attention to the more important aspects of the map, but also keeps you in a creative mode as you discover new and unusual ways to emphasize. Emphasis helps our memories greatly because our minds pay particular attention to elements that are outstanding, unusual, or weird. So use emphasis for words and concepts that you want to remember.

Stick to the rules (especially at first): Using one key word on each line is an important guideline in Mind Mapping. Although it may be difficult occasionally, in the vast majority of cases you really can convey the essence of a thought with one word per line. For those few times when you absolutely need to use a few words (such as a specific quote or book title), there are some solutions:

- Draw a line down your page, making a margin, then draw a reference symbol (such as a footnote or asterisk), and write your quote in the margin area.
- Make a voice or thought bubble and stretch that out, leaving space for more mapping off your key word. Or, with a book title, for example, you can make a picture containing the key title words on the cover of the book.
- Another way to turn two words into one is to hyphenate.

Be creative, experiment with these ideas, and try out your own alternatives.

The one-word-per-line rule is one of the most challenging guidelines of Mind Mapping, and for a good reason. You're asking your brain to do something different: to distill the information *before* writing it down. This is an entirely new sequence. Most of us are accustomed to jotting down something with the idea that we'll read it later, and eventually it will make sense. We are often unable to read our hastily scrawled notes.

The strategy of coming back to our notes is also not an effective way of engaging our memories. In traditional note taking, our minds are more passive, so we are not as focused. When we take a moment to feel for the right key word, however, we become more actively engaged with the process of learning. It turns our thinking into a "contact sport" in which we are actively participating in the flow of ideas. It moves us out of the observation booth and into the game.

The One-Word-Per-Line Rule

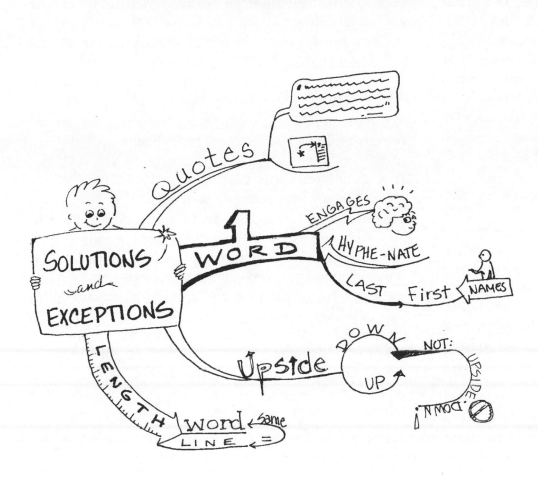

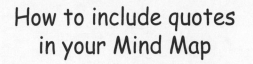

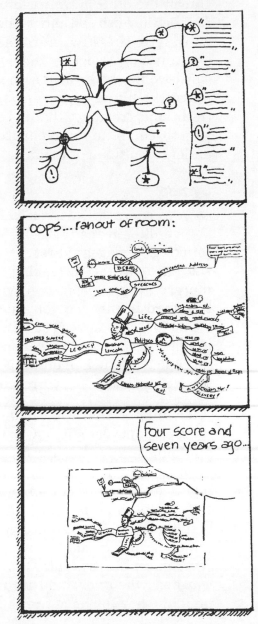

OOPS... ran out of room:

four score and seven years ago...

One of the other advantages to finding a single word for each branch is that it allows you to attach other words to the key word as you make multiple associations. Also, the single word serves as a kind of word-icon, which means the brain can interpret it instantly, like a picture or symbol, without using a traditional "reading" channel. Using single words frees you to combine or separate ideas creatively and understand them at a glance.

Symbols

As you generate ideas, you can use symbols either with key words or instead of them. Many people have trouble thinking of images at first or worry that they can't draw well enough. Start by making a quick sketch of a symbol representing an idea, or leave a space at the end of a key-word branch, so you can return later to draw a symbol. With practice you will find that it's often faster to draw an image than it is to write the word. For example, drawing an envelope is quicker than writing the words "letter" or "correspondence."

Keep in mind that you can develop symbols to convey concepts, not just single words. After practicing Mind Mapping and reading the chapter on symbols (chapter 3), you'll find that drawing symbols comes more easily. A drawn image is more memorable than words and can call to mind a wealth of associations. Recall the last book or magazine article you read. Are you remembering words or lines of text, or picturing the cover or an illustration? Do you remember the feeling you had when you read it? Hold that thought. Now imagine that you have two sheets of paper; on one, you write a paragraph about your memory of the article or book, and on the other, you draw a picture about this memory. Which would you be most likely to remember tomorrow—the words or the picture? How about in a week or a year?

Associate Freely

Let your mind freely move to any associations related to your topic. Use several colors for branches, symbols, and key words, and add dimension if possible. Remember that this map is for you. The drawings should help you remember your ideas, but they don't have to be masterpieces—just recognizable. Because you wrote only one word on a line, you can easily branch out, adding other words you associate with the first ones. From those words you may generate more ideas until you have branched out in many directions from the initial image. Allow your mind to make associations; be playful and free. See what shows up. Remember, there is no "correct" way to record any idea, and no single image or word that you should always use to represent a concept. Use what appeals to you. Later you will have opportunities to edit and refine, if necessary.

When you need more space, there are several things you can do.

- If you have room elsewhere on the map to continue a thought, just draw a line or an arrow to a new place and continue mapping. To do this, you need only to be willing to move beyond traditional notions about writing everything neatly, in sequential order.

Starter Word Mind Map (below)

✓ Draw an image in the center.
✓ Print your associations on the lines.
✓ Freely branch out your ideas.
✓ Keep Mind Mapping!

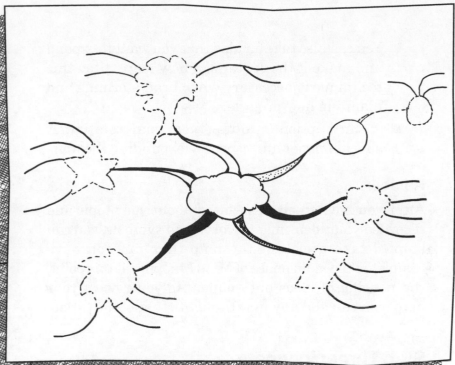

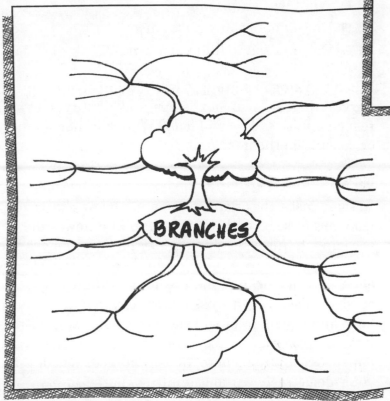

BRANCHES

Starter Symbol Mind Map (above)

✓ Print words or fill in with symbols.

- You can also take an idea that you want to expand and make it the center of a new map. Often this technique is necessary when brainstorming and planning new projects.
- A third option is to tape your map to a larger sheet of paper and continue expanding the map.

Review

After you have freely associated about your topic and recorded your ideas in key words and symbols, you can stop to take a look at the map thus far. You have completed the main phase of Mind Mapping at this point, the pouring of ideas onto paper. As you review your map, you can add any new thoughts that occur to you.

Step Three: Incubate

Moving completely away from the task—if only for a moment—and then returning to it helps integrate the information. After creating your initial map, post the map where you can see it, think about it, and add new ideas that occur to you over a period of several days.

Step Four: Organize

After you've taken a break, you can return to the map with a fresh perspective. You can prioritize and highlight important points and group related ideas using symbols, arrows, and lassos. Add codes to the map as needed. For example, if you are mapping your goals for the year, you might add a code for or highlight

activities to do each week or month to reach your end-of-year goals.

Review

The organization phase offers another chance to review your map and ask yourself some revealing questions:

- What were your objectives when you started? Are they still the same?
- How does seeing the whole picture and all the parts influence your thinking?
- What was surprising?
- Do you notice any imbalances?
- Do you need to fill in any areas?

When working in a group, this is an important time to harvest insights, plan next steps, and identify roles and responsibilities. Who will lead? Who will then support or consult on the next steps?

New Ideas—New Map

In some cases, the organization and review phases may lead you to redraw the entire map in a new order. To accomplish this, use a highlighter or code to mark the best ideas on your original map. Draw a line around each distinct branch of the map to define specific sections. Feel free to cross out ideas you don't want to keep and to add arrows to show relationships. It's fine if the map becomes messy. The old rule of neat, orderly papers doesn't apply here. In fact, the goal is to develop your ideas freely without limiting yourself.

Phases of the Creative Process Applied to Mind Mapping

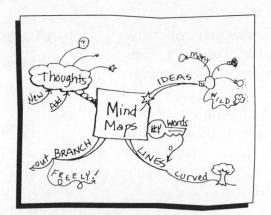

GENERATE

Draw a central image and add main key words and symbols.

ASSOCIATE FREELY!

Branch out with more ideas and connections. Don't judge your ideas during this phase.

REVIEW

Review the map as a whole, adding new ideas as they occur to you.

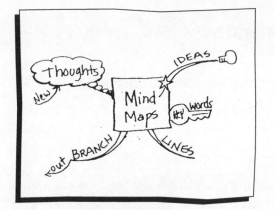

INCUBATE

Take a break from the task . . . then return with a fresh perspective.

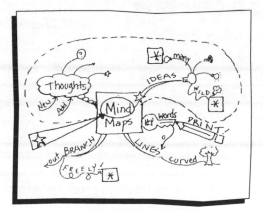

ORGANIZE

Prioritize and highlight important points. Group related ideas with symbols, arrows, and lassos.

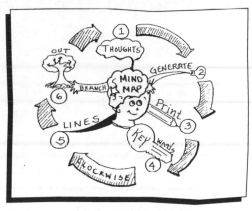

NEW MAP!

Redraw newly organized Mind Map in clockwise sequence.

When you are ready to draw a new map, you can create one that is clear and more orderly. Try using a clock as the basis of organization. Draw your first line toward the one o'clock position and proceed in a clockwise order. Use symbols and branch out as you would with any map. We are used to organizing information clockwise, so this organization makes your map easier to read at a glance.

Step Five: Act!

Begin the project, write the report, make the presentation, take the test, give the speech, pack for the trip . . . you've created the map, now step into the territory!

Sample Map: Planning a Meeting

Most people agree that meetings are often inefficient and frustrating. You can use Mind Mapping to discover creative ways to engage people and enjoy more productive meetings. (The Mind Map on page 31 is a sample of the map that might be created from the topic "Meeting.")

Step One: Prepare

Gather your materials and prepare your environment. Good light, clear space, and a safe, comfortable learning environment can make all the difference in productive, fun, free-flowing mapping and learning.

Step Two: Generate

Central Image

You can begin with a simple drawing of a group of people. Add the key word MEETING to define your central image.

Quantity

This is the time for quantity. The more ideas, associations, and related information you write down on the map, the better. This is not the time to edit or evaluate whether an idea is worthy of being recorded. (Your internal judge or evaluation committee can take a vacation during this phase.) Allow your map to become messy and abundant during this time of ideas, associations, and branching thoughts.

Key Words and Symbols

Record the first idea that occurs to you. For example, you might think of designing a unique meeting style. Branch out from the central image using a key word or symbol that represents your idea. Your first word might be INNOVATIVE or UNIQUE.

When planning a meeting, many people lose track of their initial goals. After writing GOALS on a line, you might consider more than one type of goal. You may decide that all decisions and information exchanges could branch from the key word TOPICS.

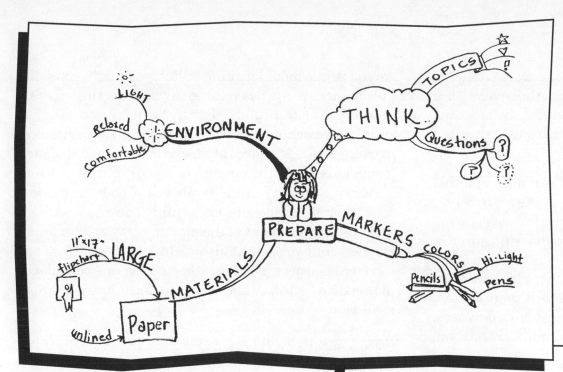

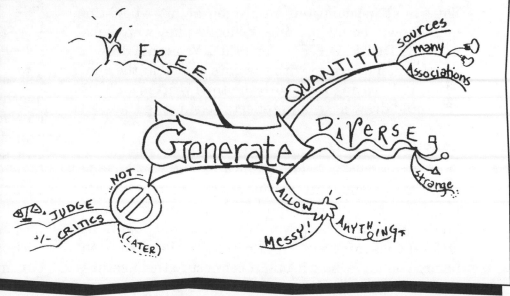

2

GENERATION

Meetings can include stated purposes such as noticing how well you listen to one another, whether every voice is heard, and how people feel at the end of the meeting. To include these purposes in the meeting, you could write PEOPLE on another branch.

Next you may think, "Who should attend?" For this association, you could label a new branch: PARTICIPANTS. You could draw a line for each person, with a symbol at the end representing gender, affiliation, perhaps his or her role in the meeting (presenter, recorder, facilitator). You could also draw lines from participants' names to record their contact information: telephone numbers or e-mail addresses. Later you can use check marks to indicate that you have contacted them.

Your next associations might be about when the meeting will occur. You might choose a key word such as SCHEDULE, DATE(S), or TIME. You could draw a simple calendar page with the date circled at the end. You could use an arrow with the time written on it, or you could draw a clock to reflect the starting time.

Associate Freely

During this free-association phase of mapping, include any random thoughts you have. For example, while planning your new-and-improved meeting, your mind might jump to a book you just read that mentions different learning styles. Add that to the map even before you know how it might connect to the meeting. Just select a single key word to represent the concept of learning styles, such as DIVERSITY or STYLES.

As you think about learning styles, you might consider how to include the basic three in your meeting: visual, auditory, and kinesthetic. It may be helpful to assign a symbol to each branch to represent that particular learning style. A symbol of an eye can represent visual learning. A symbol of a mouth or an ear could represent auditory learning, and a symbol of a body in motion could represent kinesthetic learning. The conversations and oral presentations of the meeting may suit auditory learners, but you might also include posters to appeal to visual learners. For kinesthetic learners, consider a planned break to teach a breathing technique for stress reduction.

If your next thought is, "I better reserve a room quickly," you can add a branch called LOCATION to generate ideas about where you would like to hold the meeting. Place a star by this branch or highlight it so you will remember to take action promptly.

As you are mapping possible locations, a deeper question may bubble up: "What environment would be ideal for the meeting?" So you could make another main branch called ENVIRONMENT and then draw several sub-branches with key words such as OPEN, RECEPTIVE, FRIENDLY, COMFORTABLE, WELL-LIT, and SPACIOUS.

If you want to incorporate the group's stated values, such as "honor diversity" or "everyone is an asset to our group," then make a branch for VALUES. Later you may find ways to link each value to one aspect of the meeting plan.

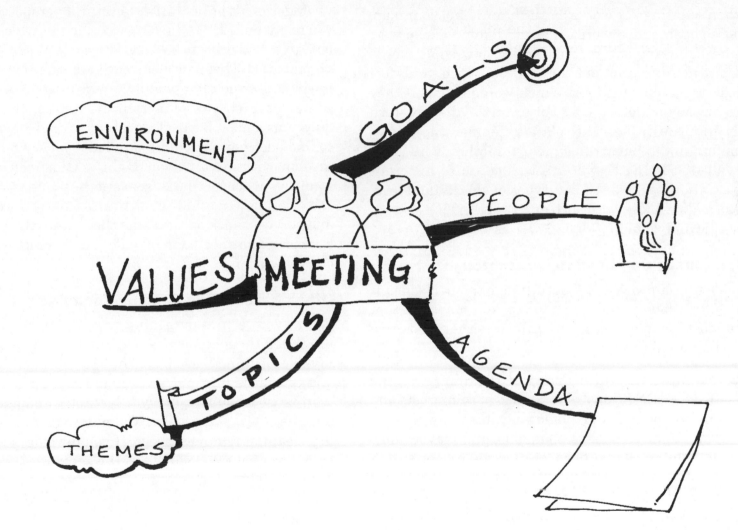

ENVIRONMENT

GOALS

PEOPLE

VALUES MEETING

TOPICS

AGENDA

THEMES

More Thoughts on Key Words

When selecting key words for the branches of your map, choose open-ended words that are likely to keep your mind agile and interested. Notice how some words inspire more associations than others. Which words feel most creative or flexible? Which words feel as if they are already a "done deal"? For example, the key word ENVIRONMENT might relate to temperature, light, comfort, and table arrangements. Another word, such as ATMOSPHERE, would produce quite different associations, such as music, types of snacks, and level of formality. A key word such as VENTILATION is very specific and would produce fewer associations.

Weird Ideas Can Lead to Breakthroughs

As ideas occur to you, try not to judge them. No idea is too outrageous to put on the map. You may find that the most bizarre idea is often the one that leads to a creative breakthrough.

For example, if while drawing the image of the ENVIRONMENT, you are reminded of rainforests and the environment of our planet, put that on the map, too. You might draw a tree, a globe, and maybe some people helping each other to water the planet with a giant watering can. If that seems too tricky, simply draw a circle with shapes in it to represent the continents. You could add a flower on top if you like.

That seemingly silly, unrelated thought might lead you to plan your meeting with a theme of different nations coming together, with each person offering the advantages of his or her distinct cultural perspective. Or you might put RECYCLING on the agenda, which could lead to better ways to reuse and recycle paper in your organization. Thoughts about the planet's environment might cause you to wonder if there is a group of people somewhere on the planet interested in the same questions and problems. This thought could inspire you to find such a group of like-minded people, who might meet in cyberspace. Or you might ask a person in your company or school who is from another country to host the meeting. You could add artifacts from that country and serve a snack on the same theme. Anything could happen, so go ahead and map it; you never know what can come from it!

Other Ways to Map Random Thoughts

While you're brainstorming, if you have a totally unrelated thought such as "Oh, no, I forgot to pick up my dry-cleaning," don't add that to the map. Rather, you can place it in a drawn "note" in a corner of the map or use a real Post-it. If you have other maps handy, such as a "To Do" map or "Calendar" map, add your dry-cleaning reminder there. If you develop the habit of making notes to yourself in the same place on each map, later you can skim your maps and see what unrelated items occurred to you that need to go on your "To Do" map.

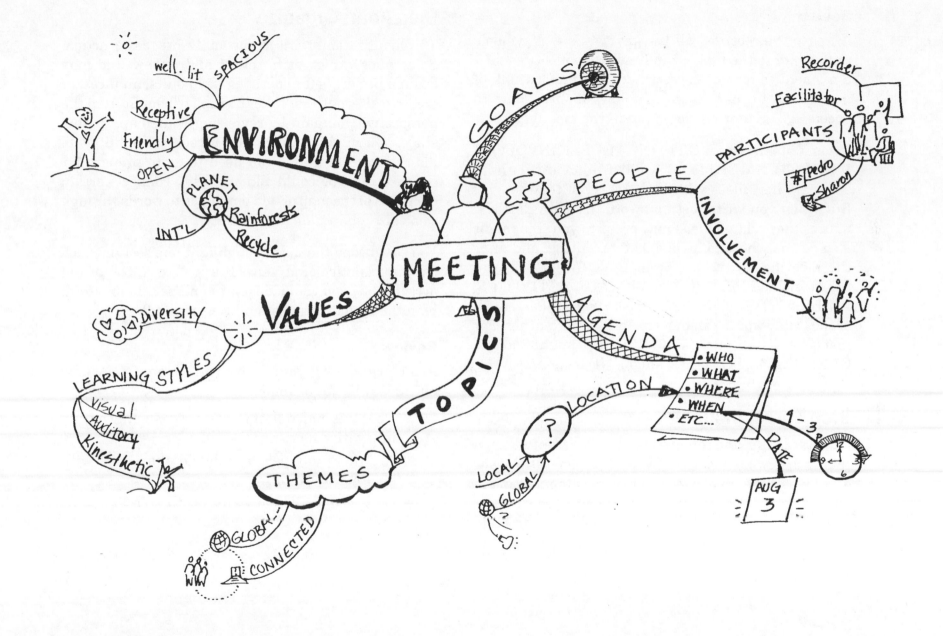

Review

After you've recorded all the key words and symbols that relate to the topic of an innovative meeting, take a moment to look over your map. You might think of new ideas to map as you review, such as how to encourage greater participation in the meeting.

If you write the words GETTING PEOPLE INVOLVED WITH THE MEETING, you'll find it difficult to associate new ideas with each aspect of the thought. But when you write just one word, INVOLVEMENT, many other related ideas may occur to you. You might also decide whom to involve before, during, and after the meeting. Branching from INVOLVEMENT, you might include INTERESTS, VISUALS, ACTIVITIES, INTERACTIVE, and other words to trigger ideas. Each of these key words can have its own sub-branches. For instance, sub-branches of VISUALS might include OVERHEADS, POSTERS, and MIND MAP AGENDA.

Step Three: Incubate

Understanding and comprehension are essential when taking in new information. Even when generating your own ideas, take time to let what you've mapped sink in and integrate. Post the map where you will see it often, such as in your office or a conference room, and add new thoughts as they occur.

Step Four: Organize

The organization step is important before taking action. Sometimes we forget to reflect and review, and may begin a project before noticing key points, nuances, or creative alternatives. Take the time to benefit from the perspective you gain by reviewing your map. At this stage, you might want to add a code or highlight to indicate all the things you need to do to prepare for the meeting. You could add arrows to connect certain elements of the map or add emphasis to words through color, size, shape, and symbols.

You could copy the map or highlight one section, such as materials (colored pens, Post-its, or an inspiring article) that you could assign to one person or use to plan the budget. The possibilities are endless.

Review

After organizing your map, reflect again on how effective it is. For example:

- Does this map reflect my goal of designing a truly innovative meeting?
- Are there any people I should share this with before proceeding?
- Do I need to fill in any areas with greater detail?

ORGANIZE, REGROUP, and PRIORITIZE:

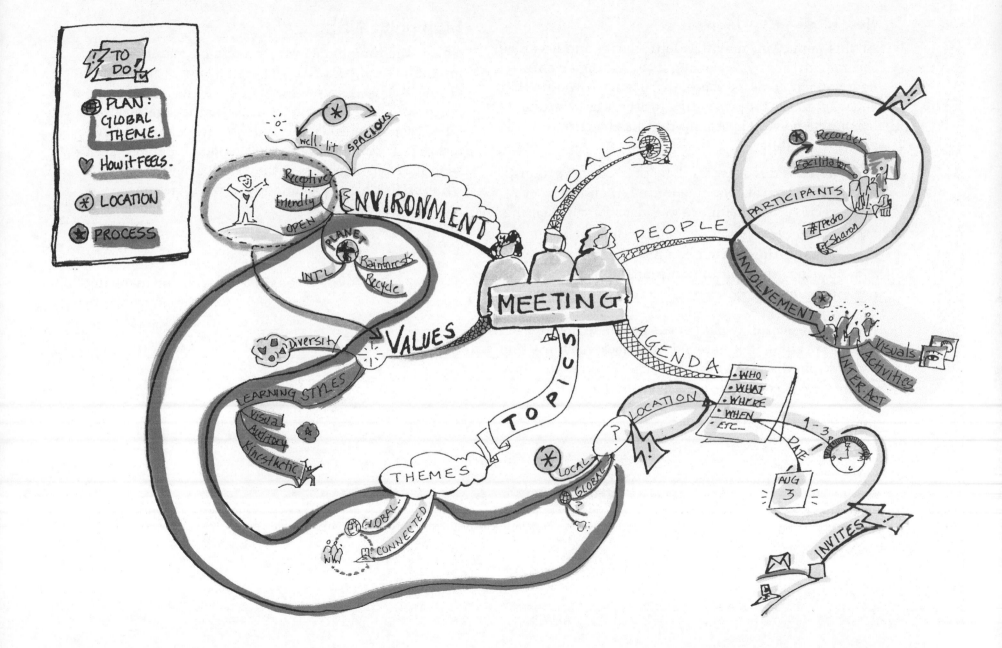

New Ideas—New Map

At this point, you may decide to clarify and organize the map further by redrawing it or creating an entirely new version. This is especially useful for maps that you want to use for presenting to others or for students learning a new topic. A map that has been redrawn is very memorable.

- You could redraw the "Meeting" map to group all the preparations in one area, then use another section to map innovative ideas for the meeting.

- You could create an agenda map of activities for the meeting, which you might post on the wall during the meeting or send to participants in advance.

Both in the overall design of the new map and in each section, present the material in a clockwise direction as shown in the Mind Maps on page 37. Now you have a map that is complete, organized, and easy to read.

Step Five: Act!

Now is the time to use your map to plan and prepare for the meeting. Create the visual aids, contact the people involved, prepare a map to use as part of your presentation, reserve the location, gather materials—follow your map to plan and execute an innovative meeting. You might even map the meeting itself, then send it to participants so they can review and recall what decisions were made and what actions each person agreed to take.

A NEW **TO DO** MIND MAP

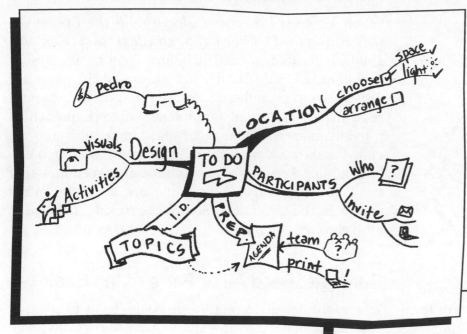

Mapping meeting ideas makes it easy to identify the tasks needed to make the meeting happen.

Out of the Meeting Map, a theme Mind Map may develop. You can post this theme map and keep adding ideas.

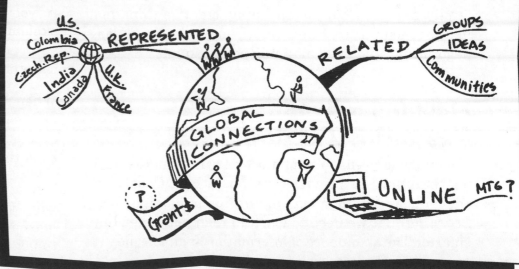

Chapter 2
Applications

Mapping is a natural way to generate ideas and then organize them. A good place to begin is "personal brainstorming"— recording all ideas that occur to you on any given subject (see chapter 1 for the basics of creating your first map). This chapter presents a variety of ways to use mapping in your school, business, community, family, and personal life, including creative thinking, making meaning from research, communicating ideas, negotiating, and even mapping your resume.

Mapping a Book:
Begin with the Brain

Anyone who needs to read a book for information can use mapping to preview the book. Ron Gross, an educator and author, explains in his audiotape *Peak Learning* that we need to learn to read not faster, but smarter. The abundance of information available means we can't read every book from cover to cover.

Prepare: Overview Map

When I received a copy of *Begin with the Brain: Orchestrating the Learner-Centered Classroom* (Kaufeldt 1999), I decided to map it before reading it. First, I looked at the table of contents, skimmed the pages for illustrations or graphs, noticed the chapter layouts, and read introductions and summaries. Often chapter titles provide an excellent basis for mapping an initial overview (or *skeleton map*). When this is the case, you can map a main branch for each chapter or section, using the book title and a related picture as your central image. In the case of *Begin with the Brain,* I decided to map chapters 1 and 2 in detail.

Generate: Read All or Parts of the Book

You might decide to read some books front to back, or you might select those sections that interest you most. As you read in detail, you can add specific notes to your skeleton map. If you need to record in greater detail, you can always create a new map for an individual chapter or section.

When reading, I find it saves time to use a Post-it note or a sheet of paper as a bookmark. Later I add the details to the map. I can then read any sections of the book that I find appealing.

What interested me most about *Begin with the Brain* were the ways educators introduce brain theory to learners. As it happened, chapter 1 was the right place to begin. (On the opposite page is a detailed map for chapters 1 and 2 of this book.)

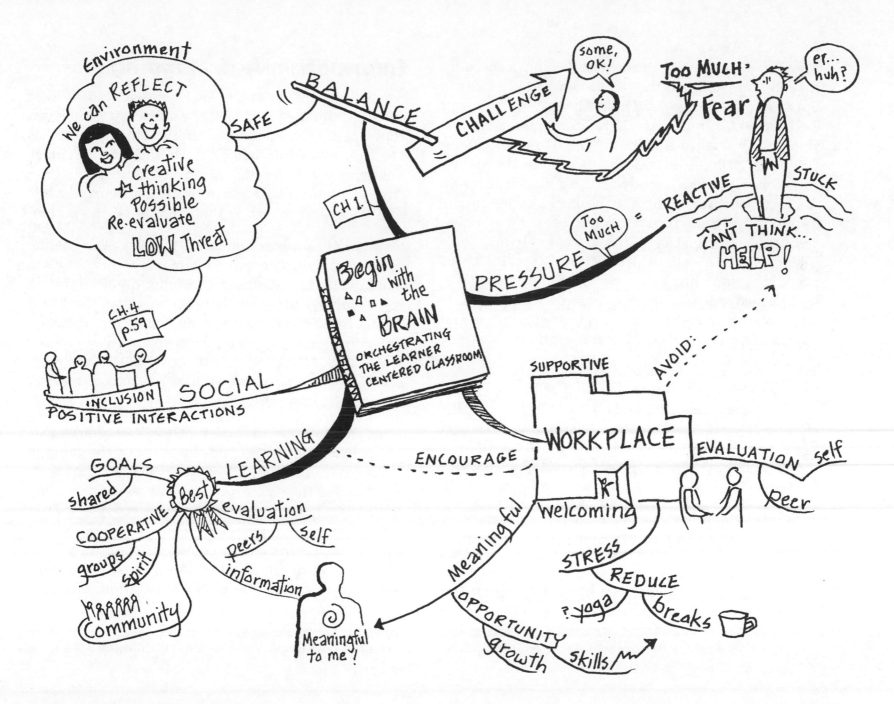

Another aspect of the book that I found especially thought provoking was the point that we need a balance between challenge and low threat in learning environments. In chapter 1, Kaufeldt quotes author Robert Sylwester's paper "The Down-Shifting Dilemma" (1998), in which he explains that when threatened, our brains respond in a reflexive manner. A perceived threat signals the brain to be on the defensive, which limits access to our cognitive resources, our capacity to think creatively and solve problems. When we have an opportunity to think about the situation, however, we produce reflective, thoughtful responses and re-evaluate the situation. As you can see on page 39, I mapped this information and its relationship to schools and corporations.

While mapping chapter 1 of *Begin with the Brain,* I came across a reference to chapter 4, which addresses ways to reduce stress in the classroom. Skipping to that chapter (page 59), I added the information from that section to the place on my map where it fit best for me. I also could have made a note, "see p. 59," with a star for future reference.

Folding the map and keeping it in the front of the book makes the entire book readily accessible in the future. In this particular case, I didn't need to redraw the map; however, if I were planning to present these ideas to others, I would review, organize, and then redraw it.

Information-Age Mapping

Students or professionals who are researching a topic can use mapping to enhance the efficiency with which they approach resource materials. This approach is particularly useful when research leads you to connections among books, articles, and web sources. Mapping frees you to wander further for diverse sources while recording and connecting the information you gather.

For example, suppose I am about to give a presentation at an annual conference and I am researching ways to make my presentation more engaging and effective. In my research, I come across a process called the *World Café,* which involves small groups meeting at tables, as if sitting in a café, where they explore questions and topics that are important to them. People then move to other tables, sharing insights and exploring new thoughts as they emerge.

I check the Internet and discover www.theworldcafe.com, which leads me to several articles about the concept, including "Conversation as a Core Business Process." I want to use the café process in my presentation but don't know how to apply it to a large group or how to set up a café environment. I e-mail one of the authors of the article and find that the café concept is an effective way for even large groups to share and explore what they've heard during a presentation. She cites an article on the website that I hadn't noticed, about a café for 1,000 people. She mails me a poster that explains how to set up the café environment.

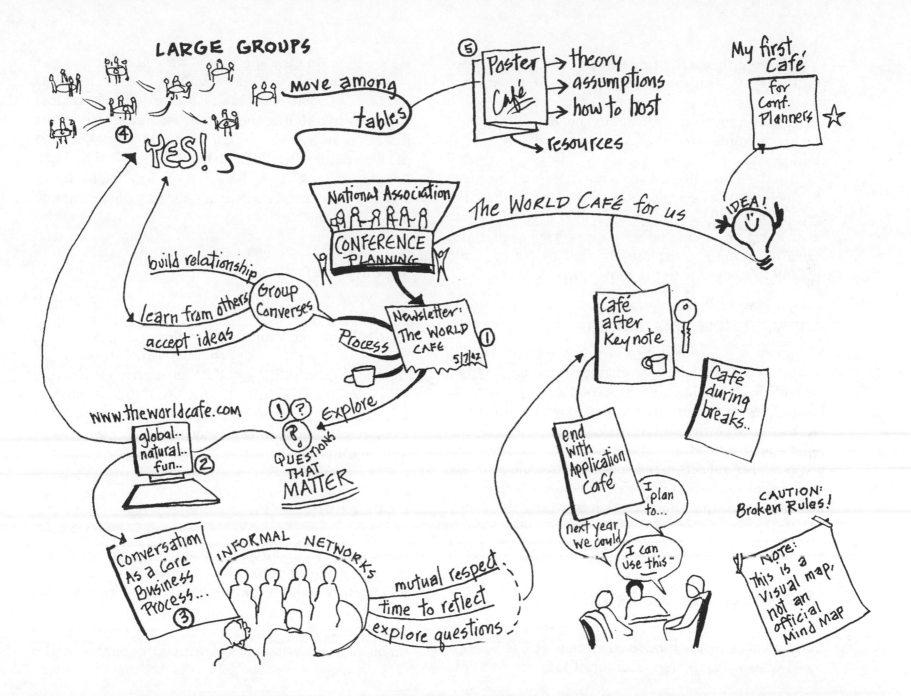

LARGE GROUPS

⑤ Poster Café → theory
→ assumptions
→ how to host
→ resources

Move among tables

My first Café for Conf. Planners ☆

YES! ④

National Association
CONFERENCE PLANNING

The WORLD CAFÉ for us

IDEA!

build relationship
learn from others
accept ideas

Group Converses

Process

Newsletter: The WORLD CAFÉ ① 5/7/02

Café after Keynote

Café during breaks..

www.theworldcafe.com

① ? ⑧ ?

Explore

QUESTIONS THAT MATTER

global.. natural.. fun.. ②

end with Application Café

I plan to...

next year we could

I can use this~

CAUTION: Broken Rules!

Conversation As a Core Business Process... ③

INFORMAL NETWORKS

mutual respect
time to reflect
explore questions

NOTE: this is a visual map, not an official Mind Map

I decide to propose the café process to the conference planners, explaining that I would like my brief presentation to be followed by a café in which participants engage in intimate conversations about the ideas I presented that are important to them. At the end, we would reconvene as a large group and discuss the many different conversations and the ideas that emerged. As circuitous as this route seems, it is contained in one map on page 41. There is still room to brainstorm other café uses for my workplace. I might redraw the map to explain the benefits of café and include it in a letter to the conference planners.

Applying New Information

Maps can be extremely useful any time you want to think about a new idea and consider how it might apply to your life. Following my research into the World Café, I might decide to map the settings in which café might work best. In order to consolidate my information, I could read the website and poster and map the key points as I read. I could set up two maps, one for the practical "how to" of the café process and a second map for the metaphorical and theoretical basis for café. Later, creating a map to introduce café to my colleagues or to hand out at an actual café event might be useful as well.

Mapping Your Plans

The best way to learn (and teach) mapping is to develop the habit of using the process on an ongoing basis. One of the best uses of mapping is planning the use of your time.

Before planning the specifics of a week or day, look at your life, not only in terms of values, but also in terms of the roles you play. Make a map with a symbol representing you in the center. Radiating from this image, create symbols for each important role that you play, such as FRIEND, CONSULTANT, WRITER, ARTIST, COACH, PARENT, COLLEAGUE. Don't forget a role that represents your responsibilities to your SELF, too.

Weekly Plan

Plan your week beginning with your personal priorities. These might include time with your family, exercise, and opportunities to reflect, read, or walk in nature. In order to ensure that activities aren't lost in the hectic pace of life, schedule each activity first in a bold color at a specific time and day. If urgent matters take precedence over one of these areas during the week, reschedule it immediately into the following week and highlight it.

Daily Plan

Consider a map for each day of the week. Using a weekly plan as a source, create daily plan maps with a simple symbol representing the day ahead and how you wish to experience it; then create branches for topics such as phone calls, errands, projects, and correspondence. You can use a phone receiver and a moon to represent calls you need to make in the

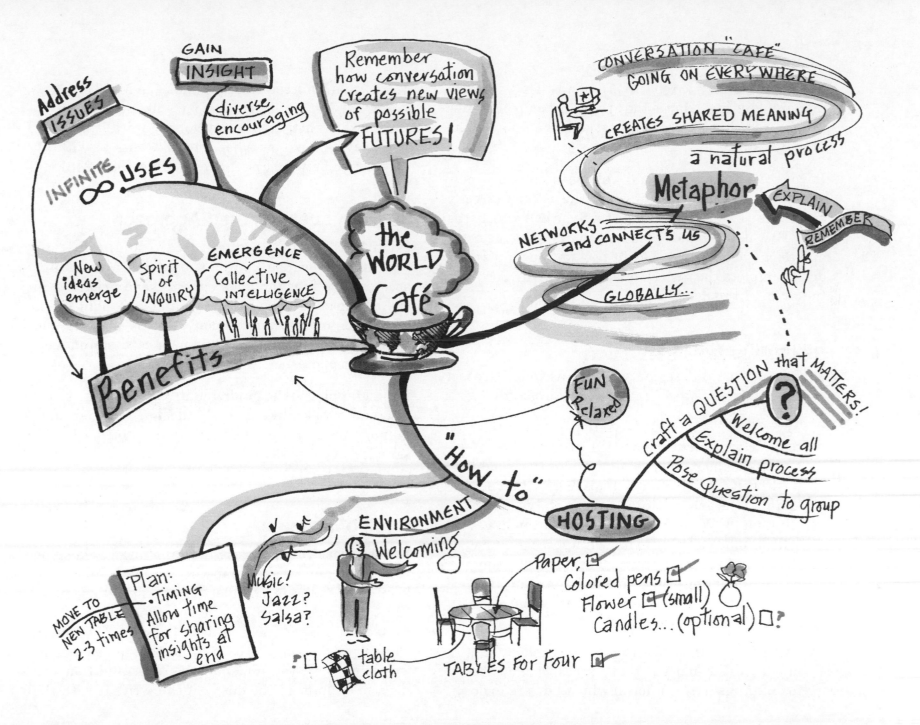

the WORLD Café

Address ISSUES

GAIN INSIGHT

diverse encouraging

Remember how conversation creates new views of possible FUTURES!

INFINITE ∞ USES

New ideas emerge · Spirit of INQUIRY · EMERGENCE Collective INTELLIGENCE

Benefits

CONVERSATION "CAFÉ" GOING ON EVERYWHERE
CREATES SHARED MEANING
a natural process
Metaphor
EXPLAIN REMEMBER
NETWORKS and CONNECTS US
GLOBALLY...

"How to"

FUN Relaxed

Craft a QUESTION that MATTERS!
Welcome all
Explain process
Pose Question to group

HOSTING

ENVIRONMENT
Welcoming

MOVE TO NEW TABLE 2-3 times

Plan:
· TIMING
Allow time for sharing insights at end

Music! Jazz? Salsa?

Paper ☒
Colored pens ☒
Flower ☒ (small)
Candles... (optional) ☐?

table cloth

TABLES FOR FOUR ☒

evening, and a car to represent errands. The value of a map in planning a day is that you can group activities in any way that serves you best and then add to the map by category.

If you receive a phone call and need to add a new activity to the map, you can write the activity directly on the map or on a Post-it note that you can affix to the map. Post-its are handy because you can write the notes and *then* decide where they fit best on the map. If you don't complete the task on one day, move the Post-it to the map for the next day.

Reviewing Your Day

You can use maps to review your day as well. Here is a suggestion from Peter Kline's *Everyday Genius*:

> Try Mind Mapping how you spent your time today. Now look at the whole picture of the day and think about other configurations that might have been possible, and perhaps more satisfying. What useless actions might have been eliminated? What enjoyable activities might get a little more time? You'll soon appreciate how the Mind Map gives you a global view of a time period, enabling you to make judgments that linear outline would only obscure from your thinking.
>
> One of the difficulties I have with scheduling my day in sequence is that it doesn't allow me to do things in the order in which I desire to do

them as I proceed through time. . . . A Mind Map, by not forcing me into a particular sequence, allows my activities to develop organically, yet I always know how what I'm doing fits in with the rest of what I plan to do. (Kline 1988, 248)

Your Uniquely Tailored Approach

With list making, sequence can dominate true priorities. Because you can organize Mind Maps according to function, it is easy to keep priorities in sight. One client who likes traveling very light keeps his week's main priorities conveniently mapped and available on the back of a business card stored with his wallet photos.

Mind Mapping fosters individuality and creativity. No two maps look alike, and the design for your time management can be whatever suits you best. The samples on pages 45 and 47 give you an idea of a couple of ways to develop a weekly and daily plan.

Book of Maps

You can track your progress, flow, and tasks by keeping your daily and weekly maps in one place. You could keep your maps in a tablet: Try using 50 sheets of 11" x 17" paper, which can be spiral bound at a local copy center. If you need to look back at information from a previous day, a book of maps is a convenient way to do so. If you remember some errand that you need to do later in the day, you can write it with the

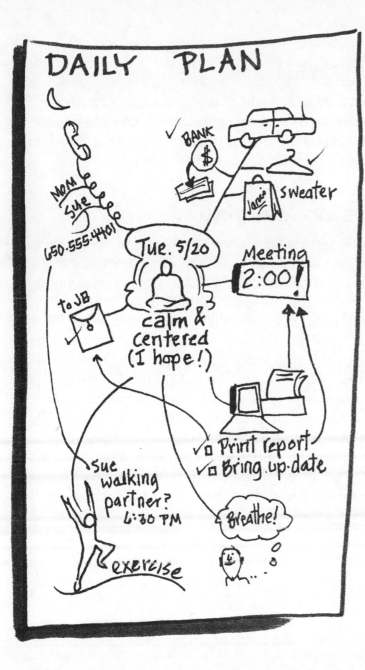

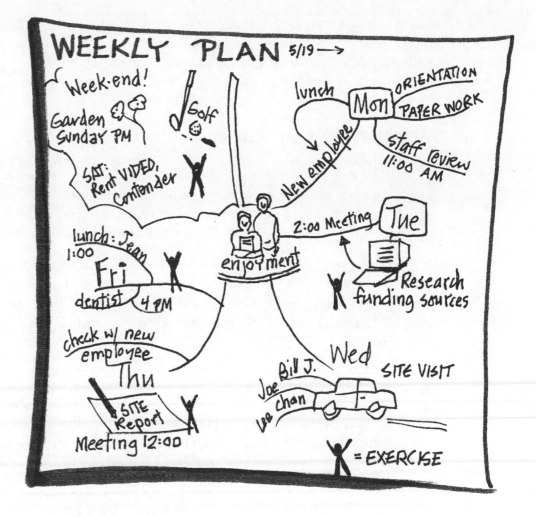

Plan maps can be messy. Add a check mark when you need to indicate completed tasks. Mind Map rules will help at first; then let yourself go—do what works best for *you*!

other tasks related to the appropriate branch (such as the car branches on the maps on page 45). When you're ready to leave the office, glance at your map to see all the errands in one area.

Mapping Your Mind
Centering

Sometimes our emotions and responsibilities can make us feel as if we're lost in a storm. Visual maps enable us to create a calm focal point in the middle of the chaos.

One approach to relaxing under pressure is to clear a space on your desk and map whatever is on your mind. Later you can return to the map to seek solutions to some of the challenges you mapped or to determine your priorities.

Reducing Stress

Mapping is a profound way to sort through thoughts and feelings. You may want to take time to map freely all the thoughts and feelings you can identify when you feel your perspective is clouded. Try dedicating ten minutes to mapping your mind without stopping. Notice how you feel after the time is up. You can return to the map and branch from each area of concern with another point of view that may feel more hopeful.

Mental Floss

Creativity author and advisor Julia Cameron recommends taking time every morning for "morning papers" (1992). Mapping early in the day, as a daily routine, helps clear your thoughts and emotions.

Decision Mapping

You can use comparisons and contrasts in map form to weigh decisions, analyze situations or current events, or look for similarities and differences. For example, try mapping the pluses, minuses, and interesting (or neutral) points of a possible action, event, or law. This approach to considering options was developed by Edward de Bono, author of many excellent books, including *Lateral Thinking* (1990). He suggests approaching a proposed action by generating a range of opinions and ideas before forming conclusions. By letting the structure of the map be flexible, you are free to set up the map to serve you best. Try creating a visual map in columns, overlapping shapes, puzzle pieces, or links in a chain. See page 135 for examples of various ways to configure a map.

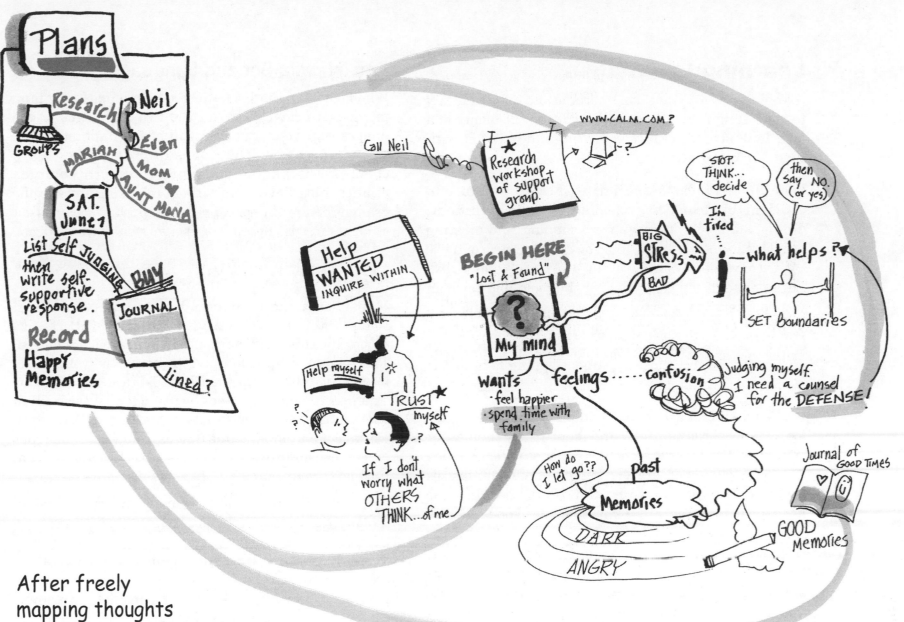

After freely
mapping thoughts
and feelings *first*, I then
created the plan for Saturday.

Learning Languages

Mapping also provides a memorable and engaging way to learn languages. If you need to learn the basics of a new language quickly, try making index cards with theme maps on each one.

For example, when taking a trip to France, some useful cards might include maps about travel and directions, dining, hotels, basic questions, shopping, and meeting people in initial conversation. You can map each of these topics conveniently on the unlined side of an index card. Large enough for easy reading, but foldable to fit in your pocket, 5" x 7" cards are a good size. Dedicate a useful card to common verb conjugations. Obtain a list of the 100 most commonly used words in your target language, and sort those by Mind Mapping to tame the basics of any language.

Rather than tackle one big random map of 100 words, look at the words carefully and identify key themes for your main branches or as central images for each index card map. The act of categorizing the words familiarizes you with both their meaning and usage. Recording the necessary anchors for the language all in one place on a map helps you quickly familiarize yourself with the new vocabulary. You can use colors to code the different branches and pictures to make them much more memorable. Try saying the words out loud as you write and illustrate them to engage your multisensory learning capacity.

English as a Second Language

When teaching English as a second language, mapping provides a bridge between the two languages. Place images that your students will easily understand on the map alongside the English words as they learn them. Maps enable students to record complex relationships and events without requiring any specific grammar. After the concepts are mapped, you can assist students in writing an English version of their ideas.

Mapping Your Resume

Maps also make unique and high quality resumes. Imagine the attention a visual resume will receive among hundreds of traditional resumes to be reviewed. The resume map may have a picture of you in the middle, your business card, and branches for your experience, education, and the usual topics. In addition your map might include areas for your values, preferred working environment, and quotes from your colleagues or supervisor. You can always attach a traditional resume to your map.

One woman who presented a game-board resume called "Non-trivial Pursuit" told me that at first she was afraid the potential employer would think she was strange. Then she realized that an organization that values creative and unique presentations is just the type of place she wanted to work. "If they don't like my resume, this isn't the place I want to work," she explained. Those of you who prefer a more traditional resume can still use mapping to generate, sort, and organize your ideas before creating the final resume.

These French language cards show how visual maps can group themes and simplify language learning.

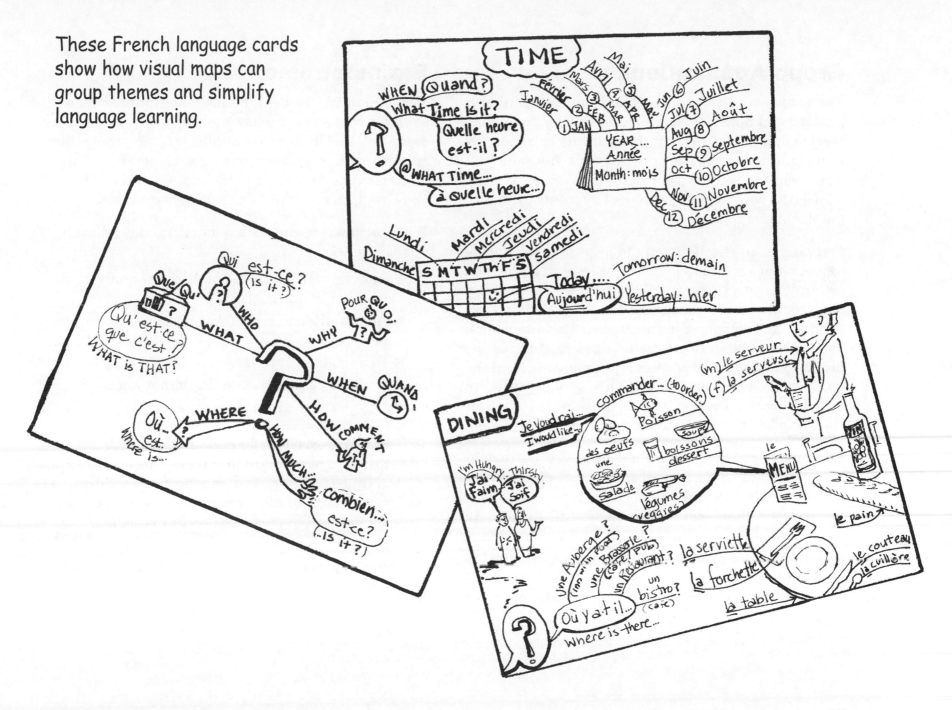

Group Applications

The more you use mapping for your personal and professional needs, the better prepared you will be to teach mapping and to help your students or colleagues find applications that meet their needs. If you haven't already begun your own map, now is the time. The map on page 21 will remind you of the key points to keep in mind while mapping.

Mapping is an excellent way to focus a group during conversations and meetings. One mapper at a flip chart or large sheet of paper on the wall can capture key ideas, enabling the group to watch as their ideas are recorded and relationships made clear. It is also helpful for each individual to create a document of his or her point of view, preferences, or responsibilities. Next the group can combine the maps to form a coherent record of their work together. This process works well for clarifying goals, shared values, and visions of the future.

Any member of the group can use the group's map or his or her individual map to share ideas and insights with others by "walking them through the map." During presentations, rather than showing slides with sentences on them or distributing lengthy documents, a comprehensive map can convey the overview and the details in an engaging and memorable fashion.

Brainstorming

Visual mapping is ideal for recording brainstorming sessions, which never follow a linear track. Maps help organize the ideas into groupings. After generating creative ideas or problem solving in corporate settings or classrooms, you can use the maps to review what you have generated and determine your next steps.

When brainstorming in a group, try the following guidelines:

- Ask one person to Mind Map for the group at the board or at an easel.
- Accept all ideas, even if they appear unlikely, odd, or impossible.
- Don't judge *any* ideas.
- Don't discuss why ideas might not work.
- Piggyback one idea on another.

This system is excellent for encouraging participation by all members of a group and experiencing the benefits of thinking together. You can post the map in a conference room or classroom where everyone can review it and add to it as ideas occur to them.

This visual map begins with a central image, then branches to IMAGES and uses them to show relationships, add phrases, and reflect diversity among participants.

Mapping Responsibilities

For practical concerns, you can use maps to establish routines and areas of responsibility in a classroom, office, or household. The assignment of jobs is not always met with the enthusiasm we might hope for. By offering a creative process that shows how everything is connected, visual mapping can take some of the sting out of responsibilities and redirect energy toward creative possibilities.

Prepare

You can begin this process with everyone seated around a large sheet of paper, perhaps on the floor. Next, decide who will act as the visual scribe for the group. That person might be the teacher, parent, or leader, but it also works well to give the opportunity to a child who likes to map or a coworker who is skilled in drawing and is developing skills as a visual recorder.

Generate and Organize

In a classroom setting, everyone can contribute ideas about what needs to be done to keep the classroom neat, or what is required for a special event, such as a party or field trip.

1. Record the necessary tasks first, taking care to add a few items that are fun. (Color codes might help, such as red for weekly and blue for daily activities.)

2. Each person then volunteers for the task he or she would like to do. Two or three people might decide to team up on certain activities.

3. Highlight each person's area of responsibility with a different color.

4. You can then discuss the order in which the tasks must be completed.

Maps do not *always* need to be filled with symbols. A map in which tasks are written out gives people the context in which they, like everyone else, have jobs to do.

Project Planning

In the workplace, you can create maps for the specifics of a given project as well as for regular tasks. One person visually records in the front of the room on flip-chart paper while the group discusses the elements of the project. After recording all the key ideas, use them as the basis for discussing areas of responsibility and priority. After the project is completed, use the same map to review the events and learn from the successes or difficulties that arose.

Preparing a Presentation

Imagine that you are planning a presentation about the key points of emotional intelligence (Goleman 1997).

Central Image

You could begin with a central image of three PEOPLE, working together under a banner that says EMOTIONAL INTELLIGENCE. The images might look like primitive stick figures, but you are a daring soul and remind yourself that you don't need sophisticated renderings for mapping.

Key Words

As you review the key ideas about emotional intelligence, you can draw branches radiating from the central image. You might write TALENTS, SKILLS, CHALLENGES, BENEFITS, COMPETITION, LISTENING, EMPATHY, and RESOURCES on separate branches, then branch out, adding details and an example or two of applications for your classroom or business.

Organize

After recording all your thoughts, stop to review. The map probably seems complete, but also completely messy. You can now redraw the map (as shown opposite), noting related themes and assigning a symbol to each. You may also wish to add numbers to your messy first map to indicate the order in which you will redraw the parts. Begin the second map with a central image and the first point in the one o'clock position. As you move clockwise around the central image, add each point, branching and adding symbols as needed. You will then have a clear map to guide you through your presentation.

Long Presentations

Even for a lengthy presentation, it is always easiest to record key words and images that will trigger memory, while keeping the entire presentation on one page. This approach allows the greatest freedom to be flexible and to navigate the entire presentation without losing sight of the overall message and how the parts fit together. If you need back-up details, create "zoom-in" or "sub-maps" on separate sheets of paper to elaborate on any of the main branches.

Flexibility during Presentation

If you run short on time during your presentation, you can glance at your map, see all the topics you are planning to cover, and decide what to abbreviate or eliminate. If your audience asks questions or shows particular interest in one area, you can easily emphasize what will be of most benefit or interest to that particular group.

When you redraw your map in an organized fashion, leaving out all extraneous material and adding useful codes or symbols, you will have a map that you can read clearly years later and that you will be more likely to remember.

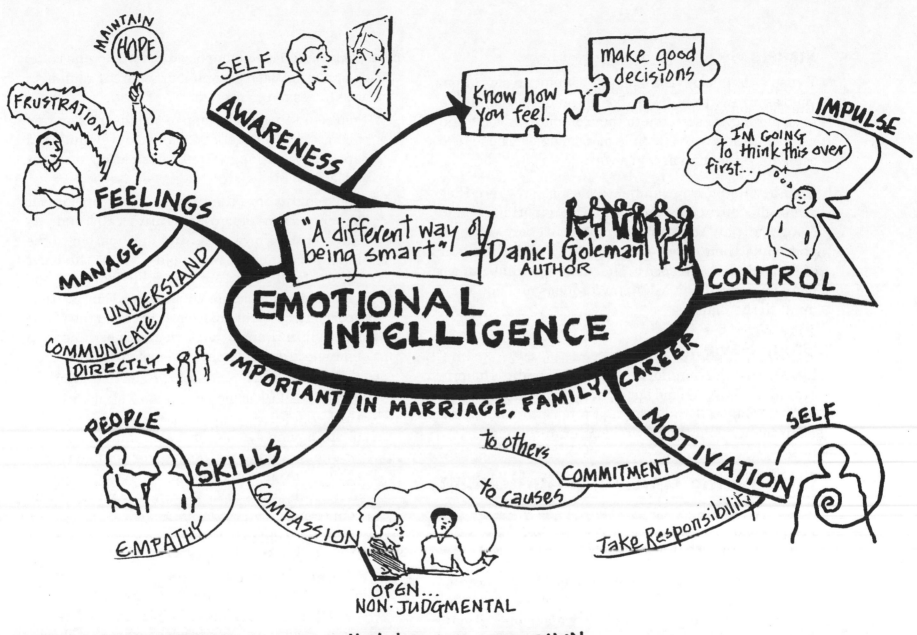

THIS IS AN EXAMPLE OF A MAP that has been REDRAWN

Visuals

To use a map as a visual aspect of your presentation, you can draw it on poster board, photocopy it onto a transparency, or scan it into your computer. If you begin a presentation with a simple map on an overhead, you can add to the map as you speak.

A map will give your audience a sense of where they are in the journey by anchoring the important points along the way. You can also emphasize key concepts and make them more memorable by underlining or highlighting *as you speak*. The audience will be much more engaged if you ask them for ideas and add their input to the map.

Group Review

Finally, use the map for review at the end of the presentation. You can hand out a photocopy or leave a large map on the wall to encourage others to review the material and add their own ideas or questions.

Introducing Units in a Curriculum

Maps can provide an effective preview of what you will cover in a unit. You can post the same map as an overview and later use it as a review.

To introduce a unit, make a map large enough to allow your class to see the entire plan. As you explain what will be covered, the class can follow along on the map. As you teach the unit, you can add additional information. For example:

- You could list reading assignments in one color, positioning each assignment where it relates to the topics to be covered.

- You could expand the map to include information about skills the students will be developing and how they can apply this information in other aspects of life.

- You could create the map on a roll of butcher paper and tape it across an entire wall. Students can add their own ideas and information to the map. For example, you could present the basic elements of a unit on the Civil War and ask students to add details to the map about political decisions, cultural differences between the North and South, impact on African Americans, and how these details relate to our lives today.

- Instead of drawing directly on the map, you can distribute Post-it notes or small slips of paper that students can tape to the map. Try photocopying symbols or using felt shapes that students can post on the map for emphasis or to show relationships. Use water-based markers and highlighters to show trends, influences, and connections.

- The map could then be redrawn as a class project at the end of the unit, providing a creative, interactive review for everyone. During the restless last days of the school year, a large mural map that includes all the topics studied can be made and then shown to students who will be in that grade the following fall.

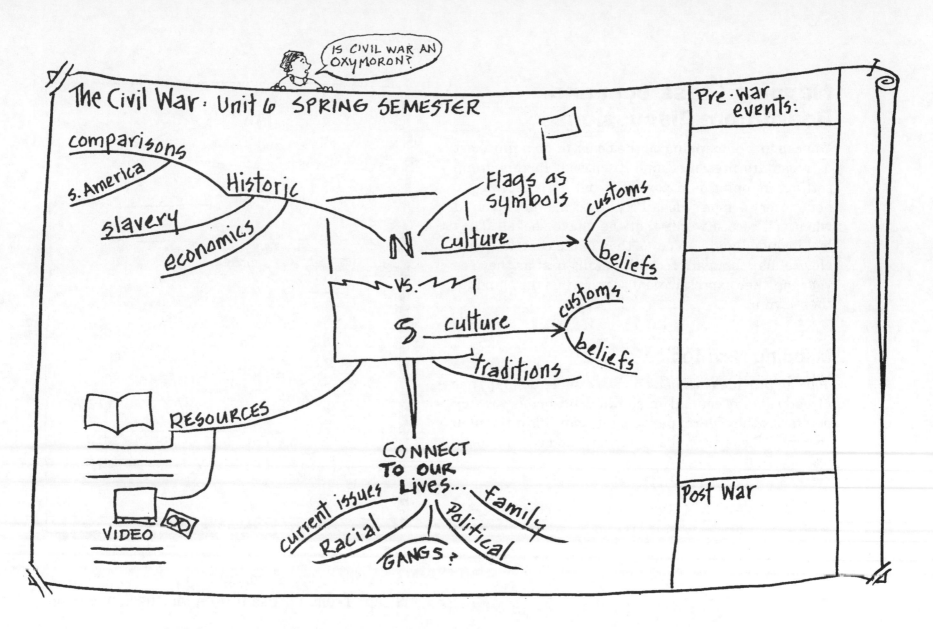

Students can write their comments, add details, record their research topics, report on resources, and show connections on this mural map.

Mapping Classroom and Boardroom Discussions

You can model mapping on the board or on a flip chart as ideas are presented and discussed. In this group setting, mapping is a powerful and dynamic way to honor every person's ideas. People become very involved when you record words that they have spoken. They feel included and valued as they make contributions. Novice mappers gain receptive skills first as they see you map, then expressive skills later when they produce their own maps.

Mapping New Topics

You can provide each person with a skeleton map that already has a central image and branches for key points. As they learn, participants can fill in the map with new ideas as well as questions and comments.

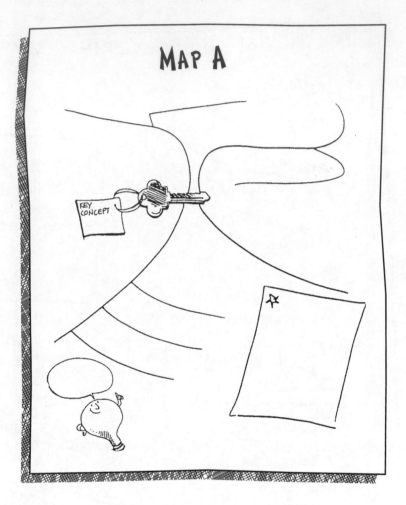

MAP A encourages learners to select a key concept from a presentation, discussion, or book.

58

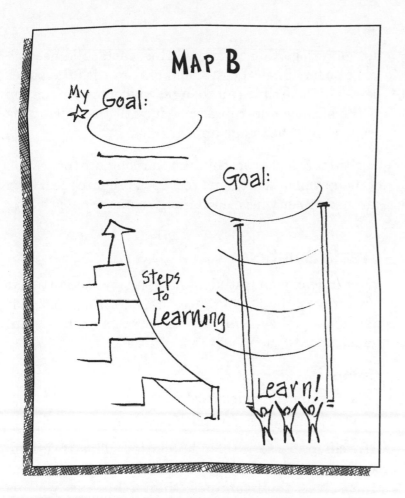

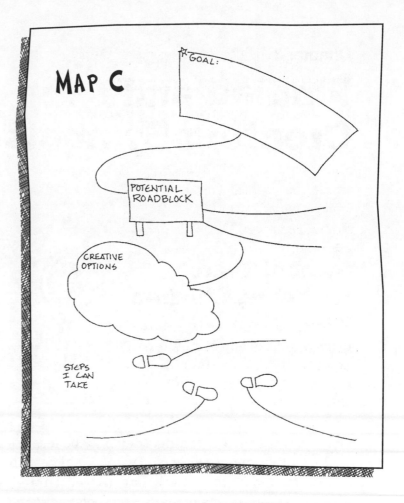

MAP B provides an opportunity to record future goals or your vision, then link these goals or vision to learning. Knowing that gaining new skills and knowledge is necessary for achieving your goals is motivating! The map above can be drawn on a large flip chart or mural.

On MAP C, there is a space to record your goal roadblocks (and how to overcome them) as well as options and next steps in achieving your goals.

Chapter 3
Finding and Creating Symbols

Symbol Search for Young Children

You can introduce symbol drawing to a group of children before they make their first maps or afterward. Often children create their own symbols and share them with each other. If you provide your students with a group of symbols at the beginning, they may be less creative in developing personal ones. Instead, suggest to your students that they take time to see their world differently—in terms of visual symbols.

Symbol Walk

Take a walk with your class through the building or outside to see what symbols you can find. Younger children enjoy making rubbings from gratings, walls, coins, license plates, and other surfaces with a raised design or logo. To accomplish this, each child needs a large sheet of newsprint and a crayon with the paper peeled off. The child can then put the newsprint on top of the surface and rub across it with the side of the crayon until the image appears clearly.

Back in the classroom, children can compare the results of their symbol search and test each other to see if they can remember where each image came from.

Create Symbols

You can lead young students through an activity that encourages them to create their own symbols for persons, places, and topics that are of special importance to them.

Materials:
  ✔ a supply of index cards
  ✔ colored pencils, water-based markers, or pens

Give children a series of index cards and instruct them to draw a different symbol on each card to represent themselves, their families, their school, as well as concepts such as feeling happy or worried, studying, thinking, or learning. You can generate the list of topics by inviting the whole class to brainstorm. (See page 50 for brainstorming guidelines.) The symbols that each child draws on the index cards for a topic such as "school" or "our class" can be compared or displayed. The class could select certain symbols that they all use for group Mind Mapping.

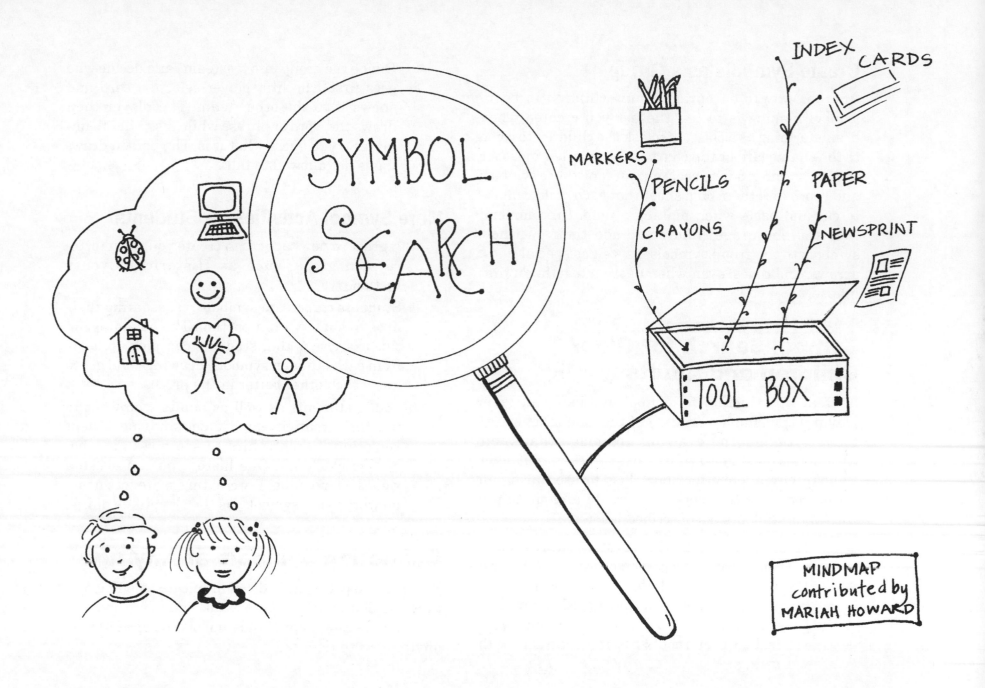

SYMBOL SEARCH

MARKERS
PENCILS
CRAYONS
INDEX CARDS
PAPER
NEWSPRINT

TOOL BOX

MINDMAP contributed by MARIAH HOWARD

Create Symbols as a Group

Another way to encourage young children to begin symbol making is to use the list you created when brainstorming as a class, then ask the children to come to the chalkboard or flip chart and draw their ideas for the rest of the group to see. You can copy these symbols and reproduce them on a sheet that each child can use to cut and paste when making a map. I recommend that you encourage children to add their own new symbols to the group symbols, as well as special lines, arrows, and codes, even when pasting together a first map.

Symbol Search for Older Children and Adults

A great introduction to symbol making (and team playing) is a simple variation of the game Pictionary. Players take turns drawing an image that their teammates must guess. If you are a teacher, you might want to buy a game for your class to use during an inside recess or free period, or create a game to use with your students (as described below).

1. To make the game, cut several index cards in half and write a word or phrase on each card. Everyone can contribute to creating the game by making up his or her own cards as well as generating ideas as a group. Include any word you feel the group could possibly represent with a drawing.

2. Divide the group into two teams and decide who goes first. The first player selects a card and shows it to the other team. The player then draws the word or phrase while his or her teammates try to guess what it is. The person drawing is not allowed to talk.

More Symbol Activities for Students

- A great review tactic is to create your own topic-related game, such as Historical Events Pictionary.
- Students can create symbols representing their lives to share with a partner. The advantage of this exercise is that students can pick up ideas from each other on symbolic drawings and get to know each other better in the process.
- Young students as well as adults who want to free their creativity might enjoy studying ancient Egyptian hieroglyphics to see how a symbol system can work. One hieroglyph can evoke a wealth of meaning. Try creating sentences using no words, just symbols, as the Egyptians did.

Collecting Symbols at Any Age

Symbols are powerful and communicate so efficiently that you don't realize you are taking in information. For example, how many of the symbols on page 63 mean anything to you?

SYMBOLS

You can quickly compile a symbol folder by scanning your junk mail. Before you pitch it, tear out the small drawings, logos, and symbols that appeal to you and file them. Bring your folder to class or to the office and post the symbols to share with others.

Symbol folders can include those you created or ideas clipped from newspapers and magazines, or copied from other sources. I also encourage you to share freely and copy the symbols that you see on visual maps in this book.

As you practice symbol gathering, begin to generate your own "symbolary": a compilation of set symbols you want to use regularly to illustrate particular people, places, things, and ideas. To assist you in this process, see the variety of symbols and simple pictures in this chapter.

When someone is stuck for an appropriate symbol, ask the group to brainstorm as many ideas as they can. There is no one "right" symbol for a given concept or idea. Each person will develop a repertoire of symbols that work best for him or her.

Concepts

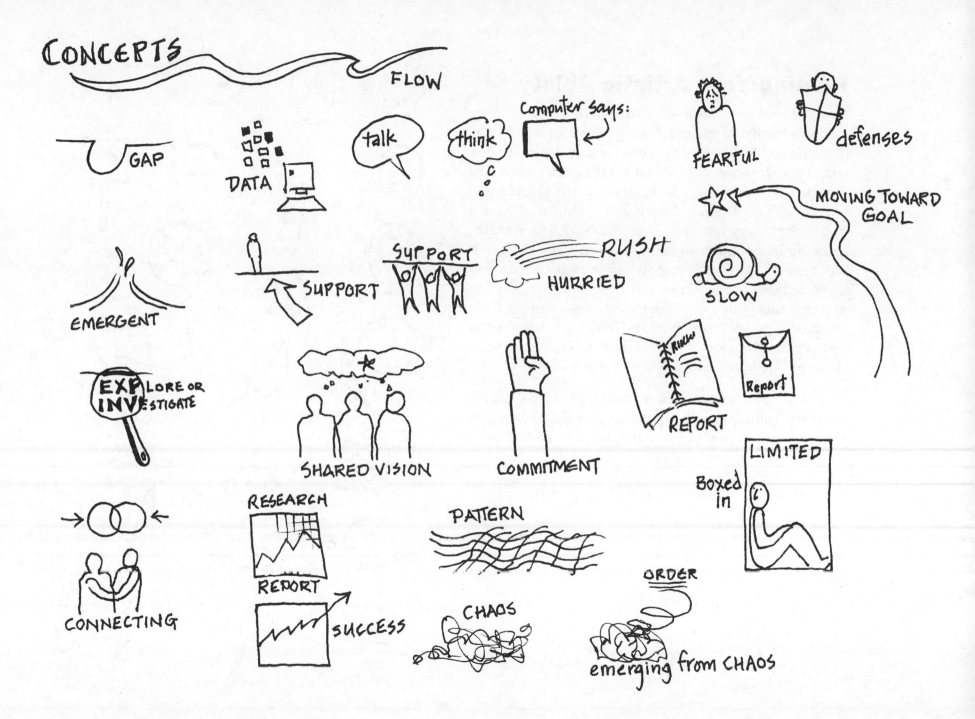

FLOW

GAP

DATA

talk

think

Computer says:

FEARFUL

defenses

MOVING TOWARD GOAL

EMERGENT

SUPPORT

SUPPORT

RUSH
HURRIED

SLOW

EXPLORE or INVESTIGATE

SHARED VISION

COMMITMENT

REPORT

Report

RESEARCH

PATTERN

LIMITED
Boxed in

CONNECTING

REPORT
SUCCESS

CHAOS

ORDER
emerging from CHAOS

Freeing Your Artistic Ability

You don't have to be a great artist in order to draw symbols for visual maps. If you're uncomfortable about drawing and feel awkward even trying it, you're in good company. Most people believe that they can't draw and gave up on themselves as potential artists by the age of nine or ten. In fact, drawing is a skill that comes naturally to very few. However, like reading and math, drawing is a subject you can learn. All you need is a willingness to try. It's important to realize that you already possess the skills you need to draw. Writing and printing your name are much more complex than the basic symbols used to map. The more visual maps you create, the more you'll be able to represent your thoughts with pictures.

For most mapping, you only need to use the simple drawing techniques illustrated on page 68. Notice that the map on page 69 looks complex but in fact uses variations on one basic form.

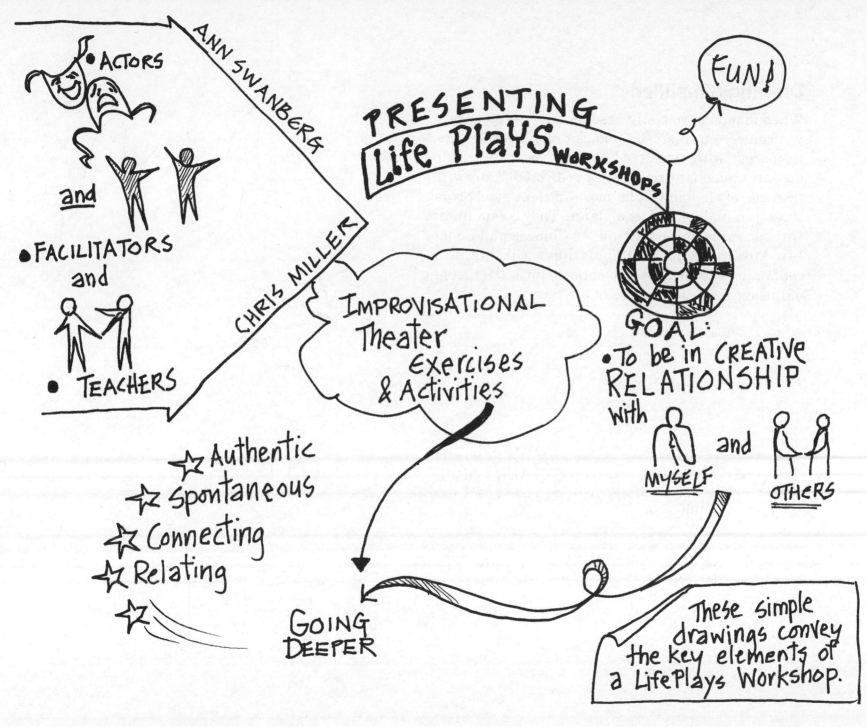

ANN SWANBERG

• ACTORS

and

• FACILITATORS

and

• TEACHERS

CHRIS MILLER

PRESENTING
Life Plays WORKSHOPS

FUN!

IMPROVISATIONAL
Theater
Exercises
& Activities

GOAL:
• To be in CREATIVE
RELATIONSHIP
with

MYSELF   and   OTHERS

☆ Authentic
☆ Spontaneous
☆ Connecting
☆ Relating
☆

GOING
DEEPER

These simple
drawings convey
the key elements of
a LifePlays Workshop.

Drawing Simplified

When mapping, you only need to draw the essence. As you can see on this page, you can represent an object or concept with very few lines. Rather than drawing an entire elephant to represent MEMORY, draw the "essence of elephant." The most efficient symbols are those you understand at a glance. They communicate without specific visual detail. As Chinese philosopher Lin Yu-tang said, "Symbols have the virtue of containing within a few conventional lines, the thought of the ages and the dreams of the race."

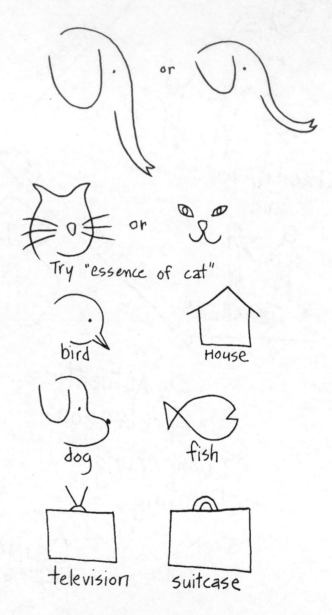

or

Try "essence of cat"

bird   House

dog   fish

television   suitcase

person   child   crowd

notice that more people, in the back of the crowd, are a simple "⌒"

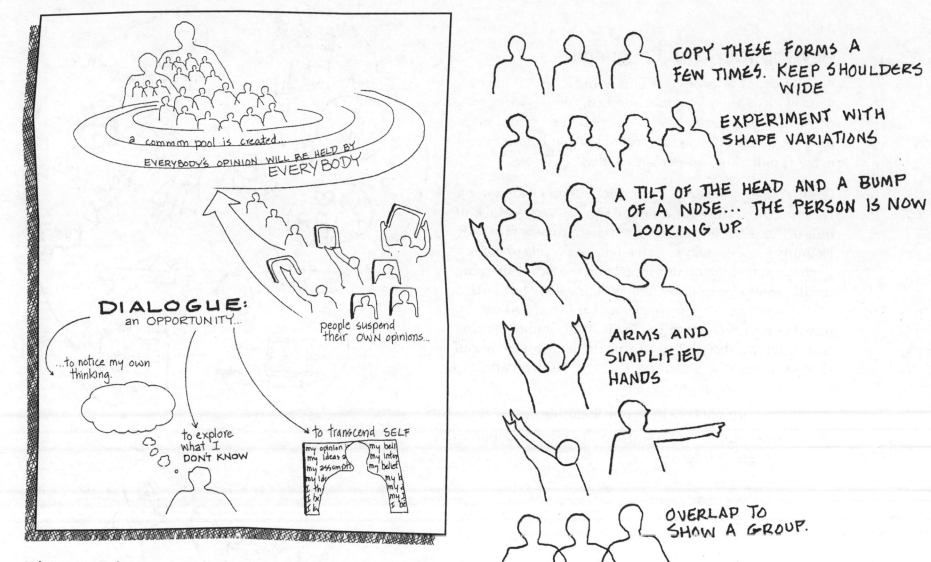

a commm pool is created...

EVERYBODY'S OPINION WILL BE HELD BY **EVERYBODY**

DIALOGUE:
an OPPORTUNITY...

...to notice my own thinking.

to explore what I DON'T KNOW

to transcend SELF

people suspend their OWN opinions...

COPY THESE FORMS A FEW TIMES. KEEP SHOULDERS WIDE

EXPERIMENT WITH SHAPE VARIATIONS

A TILT OF THE HEAD AND A BUMP OF A NOSE... THE PERSON IS NOW LOOKING UP.

ARMS AND SIMPLIFIED HANDS

OVERLAP TO SHOW A GROUP.

This visual map on dialogue may seem complex, but look again. It is composed of curving lines and variations of simple shapes.

Develop Your Own Language

An important plus of visual mapping is that it encourages you to develop another language—your own personal visual language. People who use visual mapping regularly often settle on a set of symbols they can draw rapidly and remember easily.

Grab a paper and pencil and sketch a symbol for money. Did you come up with a dollar sign, a bag, a stack of bills or coins? Use your imagination to review mentally as many symbols as you can envision for *lots* of money. Perhaps you envision it falling from the sky or heaping up all around you, or you may imagine a big bag with a dollar sign and a tiny person looking up at it. An important part of becoming facile with symbol making is developing the ability to run through a number of images mentally, selecting the one that meets two important criteria:

1. The symbol conveys your meaning.
2. The symbol is one you can draw well enough to recognize later.

70

Developing a Personal Set of Symbols

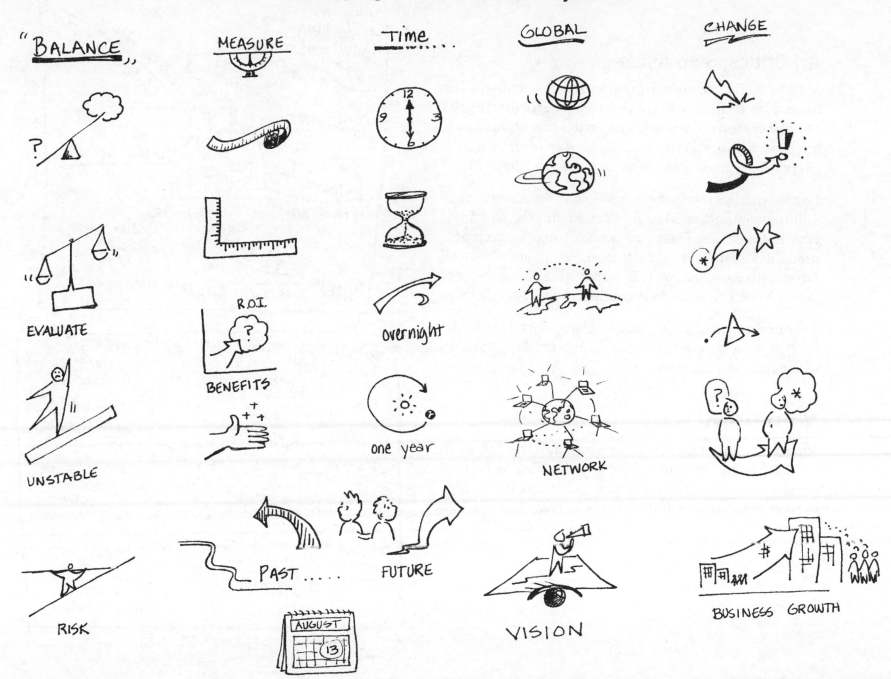

Art Critics, Step Aside

Most of us have a vocal inner expert who confirms our fears. This character, or committee, is particularly good at spotting "unworthy art." Art critics have their place, but not while you're in the process of drawing. A surprisingly freeing exercise is to make a "Critic Map."

Begin with an image or symbol that represents your judging committee. Map any criticism you hear from your inner critics. Then map a response to each critical thought. Use a different color to represent your "counsel for the defense." Allow this supportive inner voice to develop and become stronger than the voice of criticism.

This exercise will give you mapping experience while freeing you to engage your inner artist, explorer, innovator, and dreamer.

Your Turn!

Remember the last time you drew for the fun of it, without judging your work? Try drawing with that playful, childlike attitude of exploration. To begin, copy each of the symbols and pictures in this chapter.

Mapping Inner Space ©2002 www.zephyrpress.com

The map on the left was created by Savanna Johnson. The map below is the work of Mary Elizabeth Boyer. They don't worry about inner critics. They just enjoy drawing and learning.

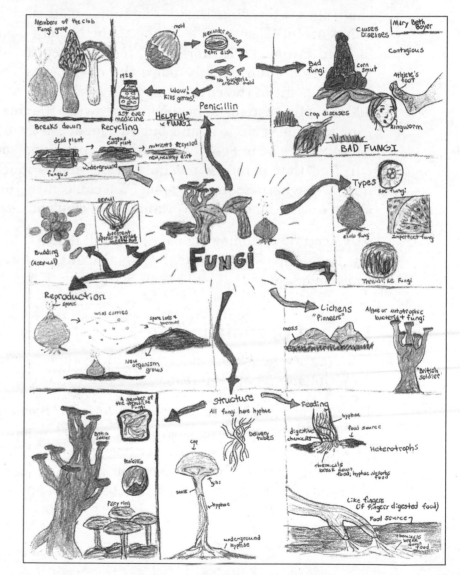

Rose Ann Smith, a junior high teacher from Indiana, sent these examples of student maps. She wrote that mapping is one way to include all skill levels. Her students are both challenged and motivated.

People

For many of us, drawing people is one of the biggest challenges in drawing. Here is one simple method that I find useful. Use a circle to represent heads facing forward. An oval will work well, too. To show that a person is a child, simply place the eyes below the halfway point of the circle, make the nose small, and add a curl on top for babies. When drawing the head from the side, a circle is fine, but an oval doesn't work as well on its own. Feel the back of your head and you will find that it bulges out quite a bit and is much narrower where it joins the spine. You can convey this shape by adding a circle overlapping an oval shape.

As you study the following pages you will notice that a few lines convey a great deal. Copy the images a few times to discover that you *can* draw.

Lines of Communication

The quality and movement of a line communicate. Experiment on paper in response to these questions:

How would a line look if it were angry? Afraid? Excited? Would a line that is whispering be dotted? Would a playful line be loopy? Would a serious line be straight? Would a gently wavy line feel peaceful? Notice how much information you can share with the quality of a line.

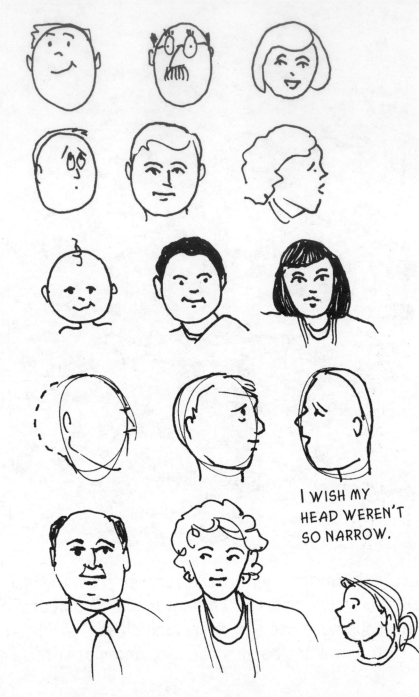

I WISH MY HEAD WEREN'T SO NARROW.

Very simple drawings can be quite effective for conveying ideas. Copy them several times until they feel easier to draw and look roughly human. That's all that is required!

Drawing like an Artist

When we watch an artist draw, we often respond, "She makes it look so easy." Part of that ease comes because the person is relaxed, yet focused. Rather than gripping the pencil and drawing from the fingers or wrist, relax your hand and imagine drawing from energy that originates beneath your feet, swells within you, and radiates from your center. This energy flows down your arm, relaxing it and allowing you to make sweeping motions.

First try the movement with no pen or pencil in your hand. Just allow your arm to move over the paper in a sweeping motion: Think of ocean waves or imagine that you're moving to classical music.

76

As you become comfortable with sweeping lines, you can use them as the strongest elements in your map, then fill in details.

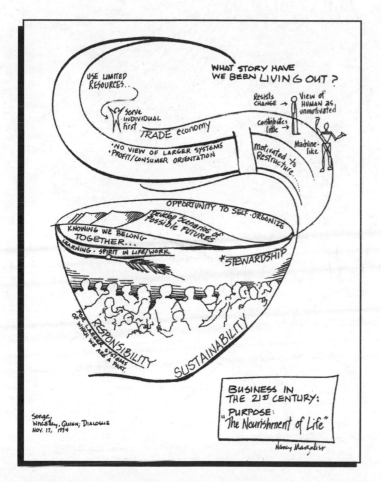

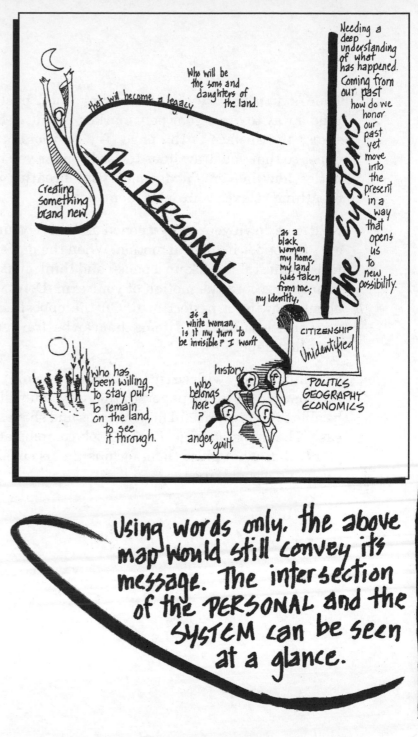

Using words only, the above map would still convey its message. The intersection of the PERSONAL and the SYSTEM can be seen at a glance.

There's a reason we call it "drawing," not "pushing." Find a way to *draw* your pen, marker, pencil, or brush across the surface of the page. Try positioning your paper so that you draw lines toward you. As you move, notice how movement deepens your breathing and breathing relaxes your movement.

Next, put down your pen or pencil and move your arm over the paper in an oval motion. When the movement feels comfortable, pick up a pencil and think of using it simply to record the motion of your arm. Don't worry about drawing a perfect oval. On the opposite page, you can see a number of items that can be drawn using the oval shape.

Continue to play with circular movements while touching your pencil to the paper. In this way you will soon be able to create graceful flowing lines and shapes with ease. The maps on page 77 may look complex at first glance, but what gives them form is the use of simple sweeping or bold lines.

78

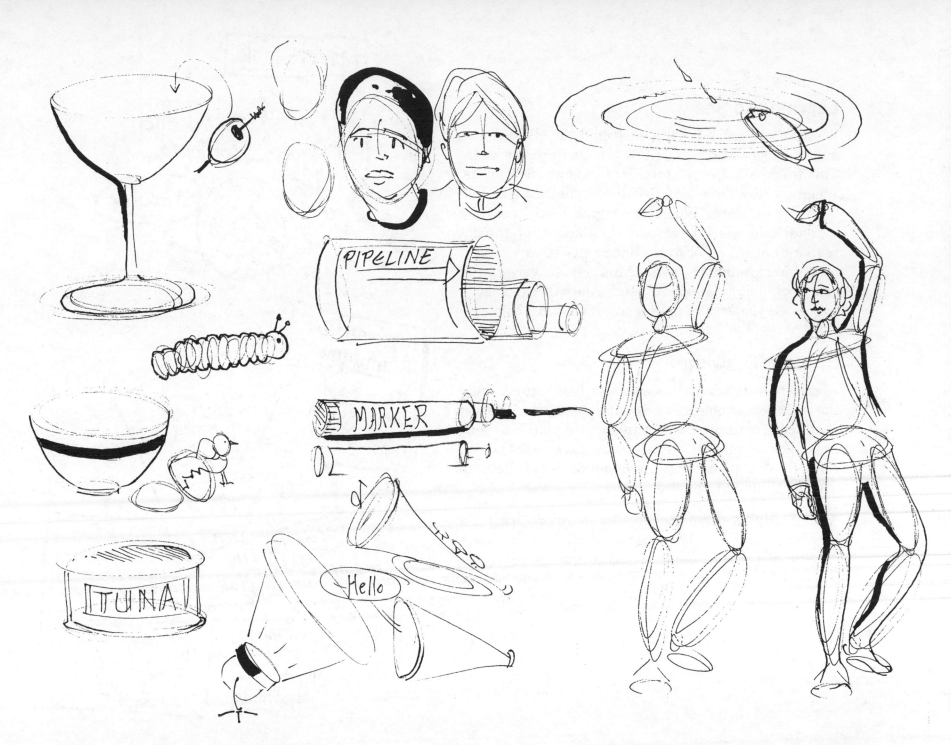

Learning to See

We think we see, but what we usually do is recognize, and then continue looking at what we think we know. This process helps us store data in simplified forms. When we think of a leaf, we usually think of a simple symmetrical object. When we imagine a face, it may be a generic or almost cartoon version rather than a realistic one. In order to see like an artist, experiment by looking around as if everything you see were new to you. Look just for shapes. Basic forms will be easier to spot when you aren't thinking about what the object is.

Contour Drawing

Another way to approach seeing and drawing is to study the outline of an object. For example, place a leaf, flower, shell, or any natural object in front of you. Use your eyes to trace only the outline, or *contour*, of the object. Look at the edges, how lines curve, meet, become thicker, thinner, intersect.

After studying the object in this manner, pick up a pencil and very slowly move your pencil on the paper as your eyes move around the object. Don't worry about the outcome of this drawing; keep your eyes on the object most of the time and let your pencil follow.

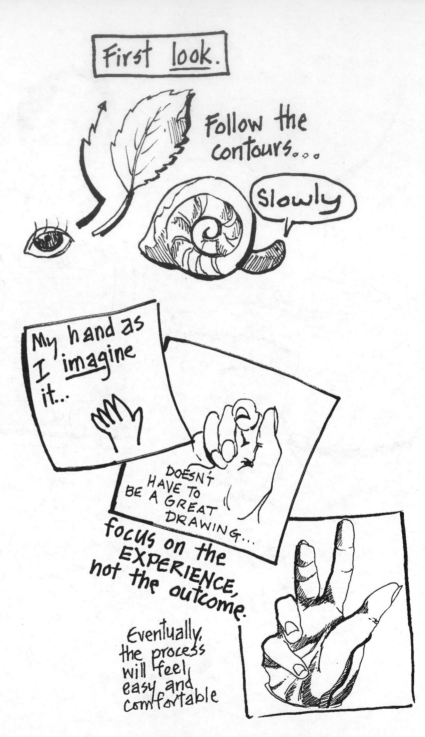

80

WORKING IN COLOR COLOR COLOR

add darker color then blend with a light color

COLOR COLOR COLOR

TRY TOMBO BRAND markers, available at art supply stores

pen end   and   BRUSH end

Some colors can be blended or overlapped.

Add color for emphasis to a black & white map.

July 22

Shadows on one side and bottom

Markers provide a variety of skin tones.

then why is my face BLUE?

NOTICE that a few colors are often more effective than many.

Begin figures with light colors

Build idea with darker tone. Detail is not needed

but you can add it with a third color.

All of our illustrations are colored with WATER-BASE MARKERS!

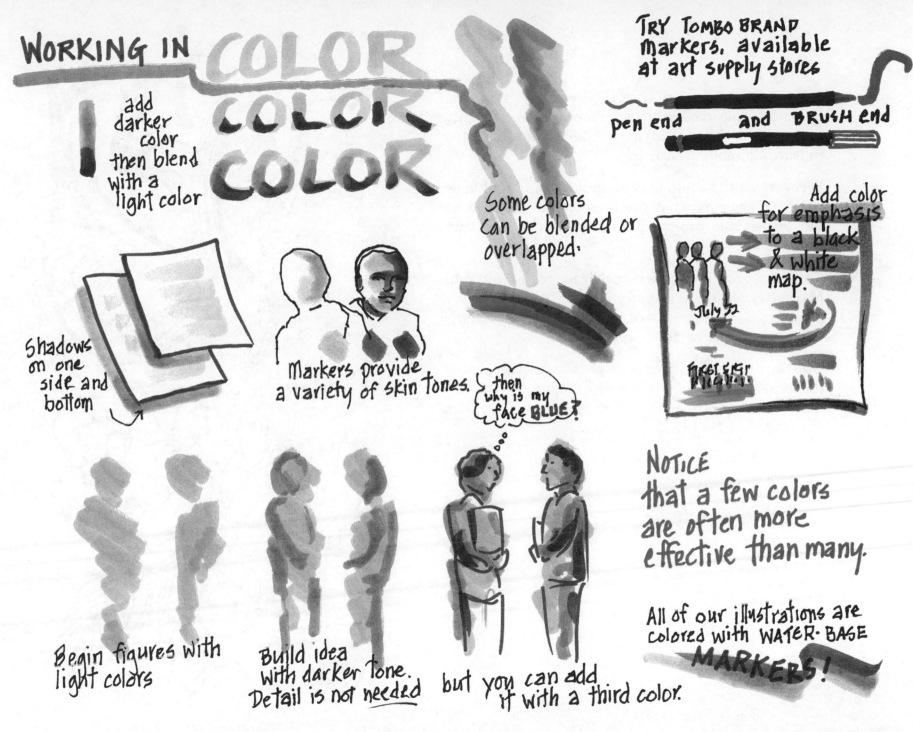

Allow yourself time so that the process is slow and becomes almost meditative. This process of really looking at an object, studying it carefully, is a vital step in learning realistic drawing.

Focusing on the contour of an actual object will keep you from drawing what you *imagine* the object looks like and enable you to discover its unique form and variations.

This approach is detailed in Nicolaides (1990) and Margulies (1991). Even if you don't want to study realistic drawing, you can use the slow contour approach to copy cartoons and symbols.

On this page and subsequent pages are examples of the forms and shapes that you can create with the free movement technique, as well as examples of contour drawing.

Mapping Inner Space ©2002 www.zephyrpress.com

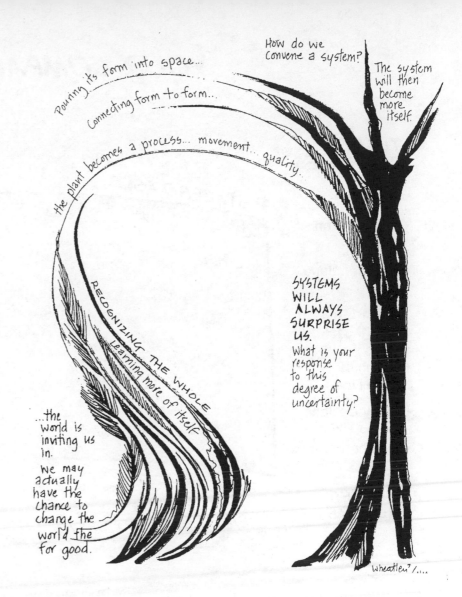

Above is a map created during a learning café on the topic of women's leadership styles for the Athena Conference. The café question was "How can we apply what we just heard during the keynote address?" The form of the woman is a stylized version, easier to create after practicing contour drawing.

One large bold image can form the central focus for your map. Above, the swaying tree relates to Meg Wheatley's presentation on systems and patterns in nature. The tree is formed with free-flowing lines.

YOUR COMPANY'S GAMEPLAN

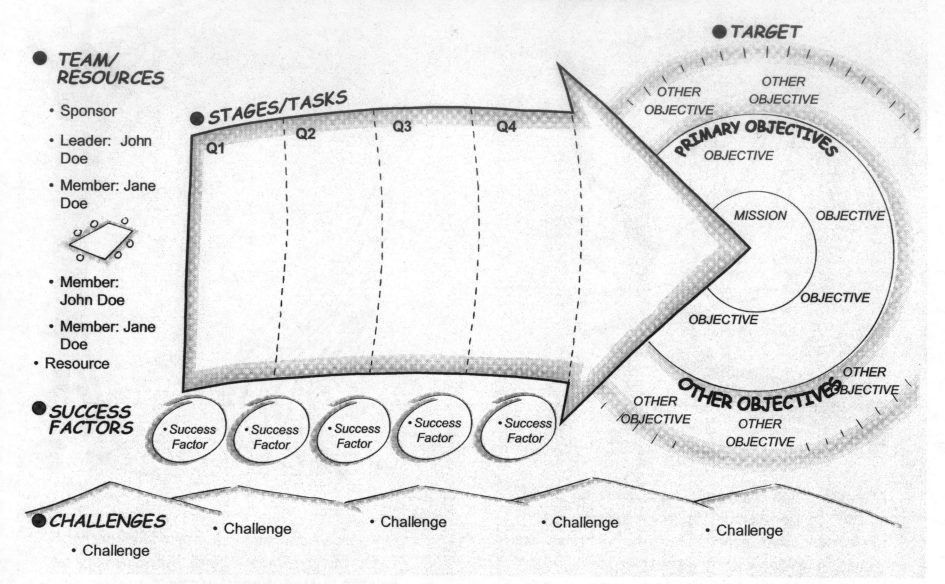

This visual portrait of a team and its resources presents a clear target and outlines strategies to reach goals and objectives. (Used with permission.)

Mapping Inner Space ©2002 www.zephyrpress.com

Maps can convey cycles and spirals that represent various processes. With or without elaborately drawn people, the map below suggests the way in which conversations can move through an organization, creating knowledge.

TEAM LEARNING CYCLE

COORDINATED ACTION

JOINT PLANNING

PUBLIC REFLECTION

SHARED MEANING

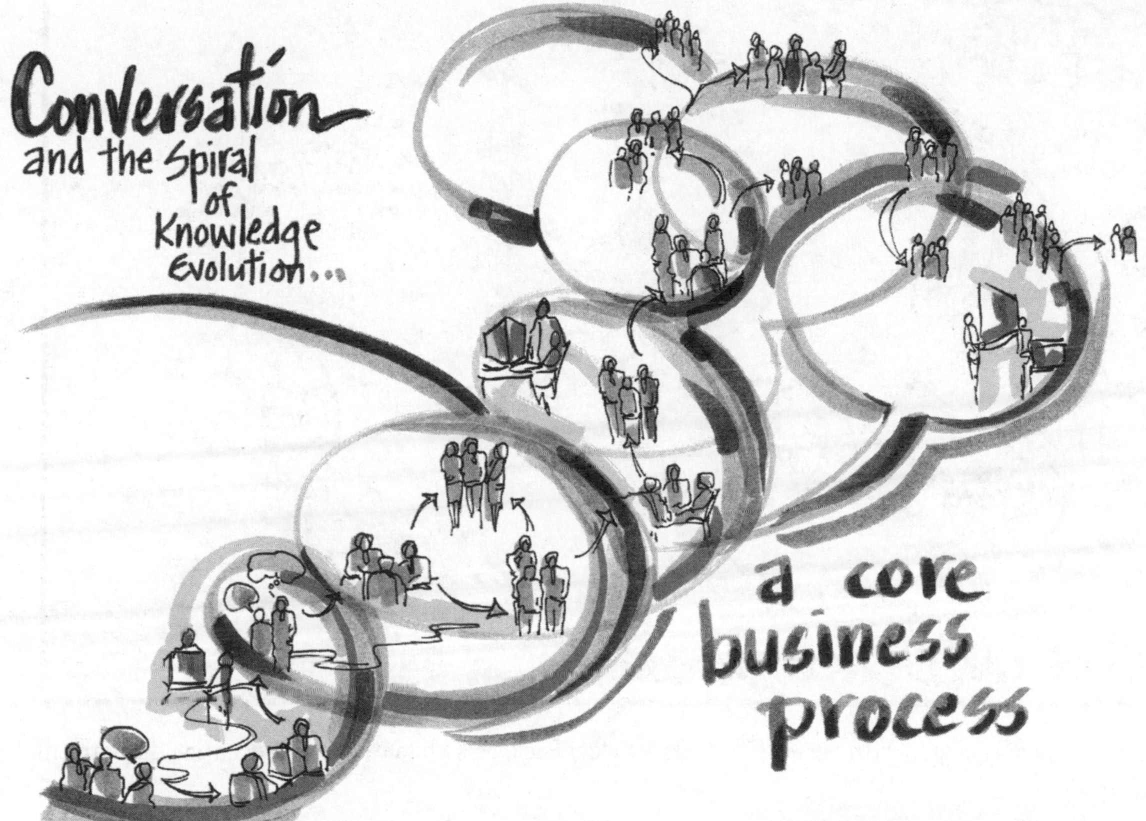

Conversation
and the Spiral
of
Knowledge
Evolution...

a core business process

The cycle of learning can take many forms: "Plan-Act-Reflect-Revise" is one such cycle. Above, the cycle relates to team learning.

> "All of art history stands available to be tapped for the best visual metaphors and structures to enable companies to see and feel their visions."
>
> —Chrisann Brennan, Chrysanthemum Design, San Francisco

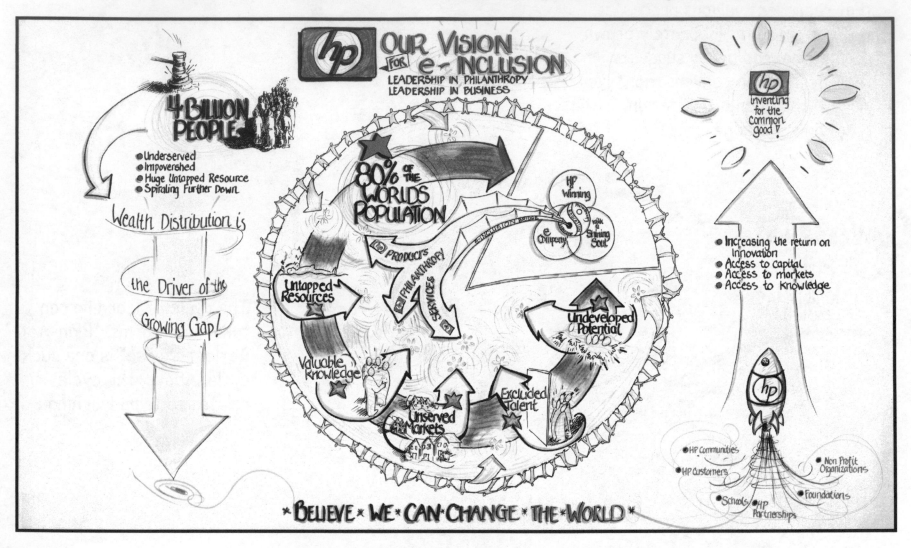

Map by Chrisann Brennan. Included with permission from Hewlett Packard's philanthropy & education department.

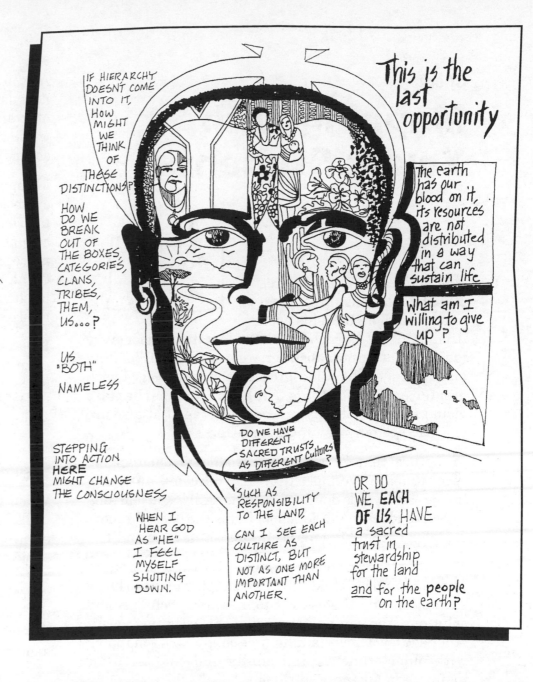

A shape, such as the outline of a head, can become the format for a visual map— from simple to complex.

Chapter 4
Mapping with Young Students

Rudolf Arnheim explores the relationship of visual images to thought in his book *Art and Visual Perception* (1983). He states that for every idea, no matter how abstract, we have a corresponding visual image. The mind processes visual images with greater ease than words, Arnheim explains, because visual images not only precede language but also are shared with our prehuman ancestors.

It's natural that we can easily introduce visual mapping techniques to young children. The combination of images and words develops reading skills. And learning to record ideas in grade school forms the basis for more complex note-taking and thinking skills later in life.

This chapter includes a number of ways to introduce Mind Mapping to children, from mapping to get to know each other and themselves to mapping problems and solutions. You can adjust most of the activities to suit other age levels, even adults. (See chapter 5 for mapping with older students and adults and chapter 6 for mapping in business settings.)

As you have seen, Mind Mapping uses key words and does not require the use of phrases, or even a knowledge of grammar. Thus, children who haven't developed writing skills and students for whom English is a second language can use mapping successfully.

Mapping capitalizes on a child's delight in color, symbols, and imagery. The use of symbols, such as stars, hearts, and faces, gives children the experience of communicating ideas on paper before moving to the more complex task of writing. Because symbolic thinking using visual images precedes spoken language, it remains important long after we learn to read and write.

If we see the purpose of written language as a tool for recording and communicating our inner world and ideas, why not motivate and excite children with an intriguing yet simple method to convey what they know and how they feel?

Demonstrating

When I visit elementary schools to teach mapping, I explain that I am going to show students a new and exciting way to write ideas. I ask them to think of a subject that interests them. The topics they choose may range from soccer to science. The only qualification is that they must know enough about the subject to tell me about it. For instance, one class I spoke to selected science as a favorite subject. (I hope they will say the same when they reach 10th grade!)

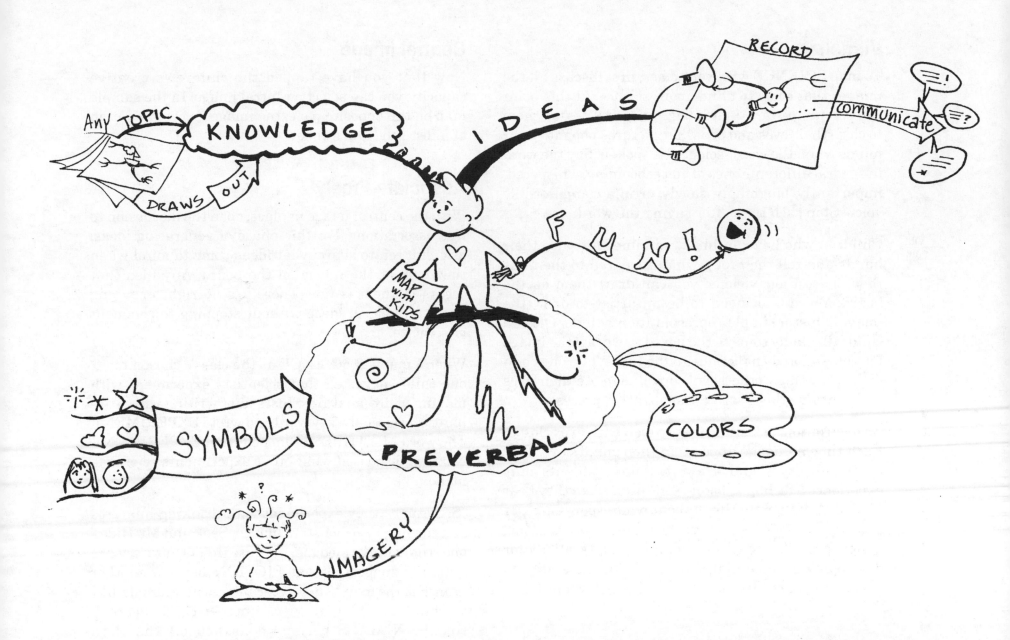

Any TOPIC → KNOWLEDGE · DRAWS OUT · IDEAS · RECORD · communicate · FUN! · MAP WITH KIDS · SYMBOLS · PREVERBAL · IMAGERY · COLORS

Visualize

To map SCIENCE with your class, first discuss all the images that come to mind about science. At this point you can jump-start their imaginations by asking them to close their eyes and see what pictures pop into their minds when the word "science" is spoken. Say the word in several different tones of voice: booming, whispered, importantly, laughingly, slowly, or in a computer-like voice. Stop each time after saying the word.

Children who have an image in mind can raise their hands and tell the group what appeared to them. As they share their visions, you can draw them on the board. You do not need to be an artist to draw the images. Just a simple representation will do. Often a child will gladly come to the board and draw the image for you. Colored chalk adds to the fun. While one child draws an image, others can copy it, or close their eyes and continue the creative visualization process.

As a variation, ask students to listen with eyes closed. Each time an image appears in their mind's eye, they open their eyes and draw it. Some students may experience a feeling or bodily sensation when they hear a word. Ask them to think about what color, shape, or texture this feeling or word has. This process alone, which precedes teaching mapping, is excellent for developing an essential learning skill: the ability to visualize and to take note of your *inner* responses.

Central Image

Now that you have tapped the children's creative capacity, you can select a central image. In the sample map on the opposite page, the image is a combination of a test tube and a robot.

Associate Freely

With the central image in place, open the discussion to free associations. For this phase of generating ideas, ask children to share what ideas come to mind when they look at the image on the board. Any idea that occurs to them is fine. There are no right or wrong answers. List all ideas without stopping to comment or criticize.

When I mapped SCIENCE as the class's chosen topic, one child suggested that scientists experiment with making weird mixtures. Instead of writing the entire phrase, I selected a key word and wrote EXPERIMENT. The word MIXTURES branched from EXPERIMENT. Next we discussed what other experiments scientists make.

"Sometimes they experiment with drinking mixtures and turning into monsters like Dr. Seek and Mr. Hide," one student informed me. Because that is more science fiction, I suggested that FICTION become another branch of the map. "They experiment with animals, like teaching a monkey to type," another child reported. Good! ANIMALS became a branch off the word

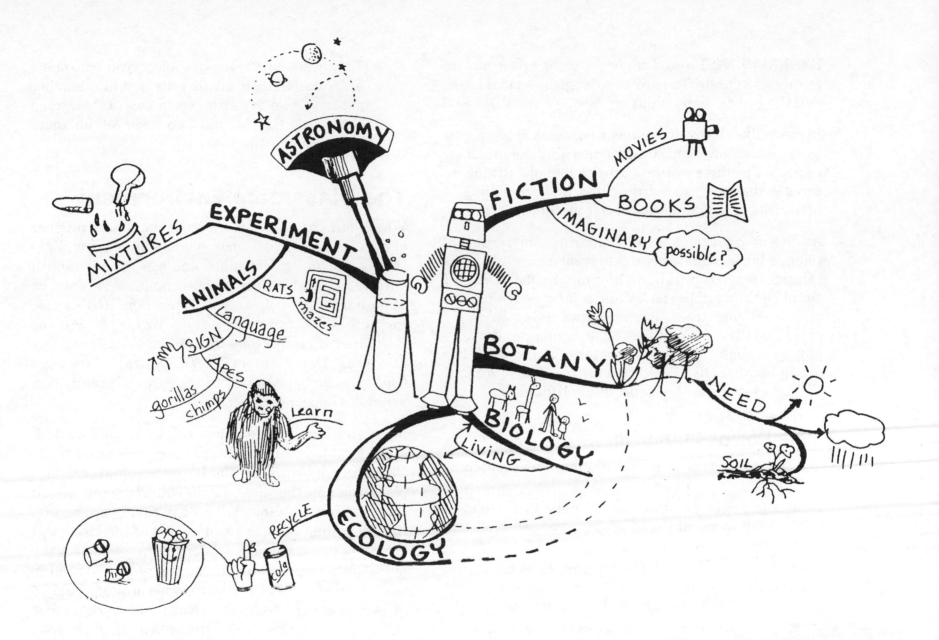

ASTRONOMY

FICTION
MOVIES
BOOKS
IMAGINARY
Possible?

EXPERIMENT
MIXTURES

ANIMALS
RATS mazes
Language
SIGN
Apes
gorillas chimps
Learn

BOTANY
NEED
SOIL

BIOLOGY
Living

RECYCLE
Cola

ECOLOGY

EXPERIMENT. I asked them for ideas about how to represent a gorilla. The arms are long, the head is large, and the body is hairy. I did my best.

In cases like this, you can feel free to ask students for assistance. More important, your willingness to draw imperfect pictures on the board is a real plus. Students can see that you are learning, too, and are willing to take risks or ask for assistance from them.

As the map on page 91 demonstrates, my group of science buffs came up with a great range of topics related to science. When they mentioned plants, I supplied the word BOTANY and reinforced it with lots of flowers and trees. For studying living things, I explained BIOLOGY. At that point I explained that any key word could become the center of a new map. For example, BIOLOGY could be a central image, with all the associations to that topic filling the board.

More Demonstration Ideas

You can repeat this demonstration process as often as you like.

- You might create a second map as a group of children recall the elements of a story that you read to them.
- As you explain a topic, ask your class to suggest the next branch or advise you where the next piece of information fits best on the map.
- Older children can review all the facts of a subject they recently studied while one of them maps on the chalkboard or a large piece of paper.

- To preview or review a subject, you can make maps on large sheets or rolls of white butcher paper to display in the room (see "Introducing Units in a Curriculum," on page 56, for more details and examples).

The Classroom Environment

When your goal is to generate the maximum number of creative ideas, take time to create an environment that is relaxing, comfortable, and safe. To accomplish this, you might play some classical music or instrumentals such as the Windham Hill series. Pachelbel's *Canon,* Handel's *Water Music,* or Beethoven's *Emperor Concerto* are excellent for creative exercises. Don Campbell's *The Mozart Effect for Children* (2000) is an inspiring source of information about the impact of music.

Make sure that everyone has sufficient table or desk space for a large sheet of paper and several markers. Children might find it handy to keep markers in a plastic cup on the table. Some children work best if they are not at a table, but rather sitting or lying on the floor. Mind Mapping can be one of the classroom activities in which each student is free to select the position that works best. Those students who need to take frequent breaks or like to move around could be allowed to get up, stretch, and look at the work of other children. When possible, let students experiment with standing at an easel or working with colored chalk on the board.

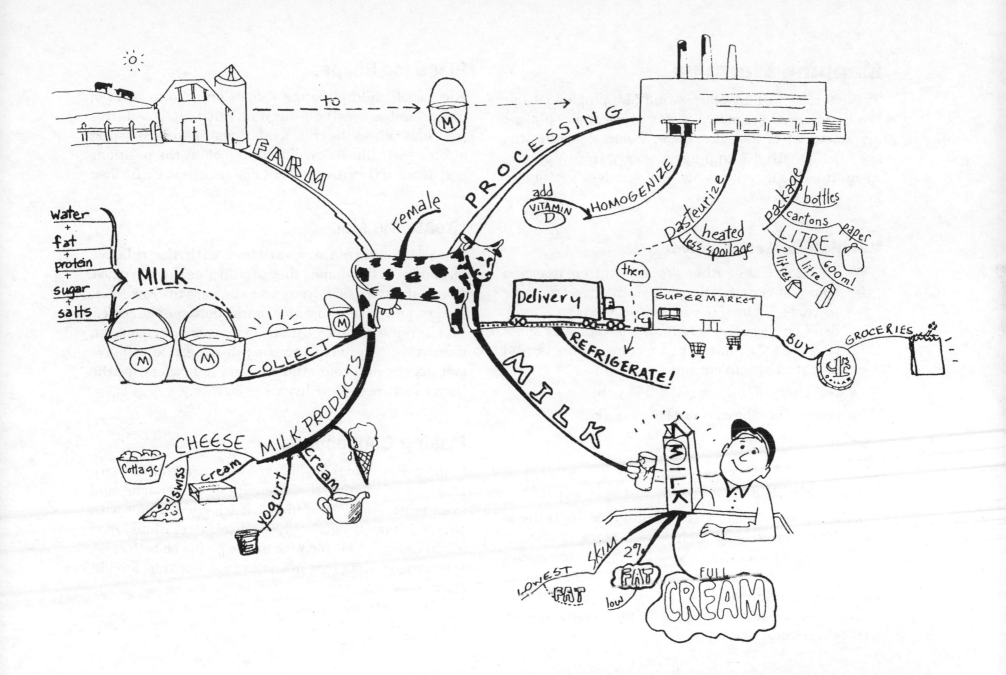

FARM

to

PROCESSING

Female

add VITAMIN D

HOMOGENIZE

pasteurize
heated
less spoilage

package
bottles
cartons
paper
LITRE
2 litres
1 litre
600 ml

Water
+
fat
+
protein
+
sugar
+
salts

MILK

COLLECT

then

Delivery

SUPERMARKET

MILK

REFRIGERATE!

BUY

GROCERIES

MILK PRODUCTS

CHEESE

Cottage

Swiss

cream

cream

yogurt

MILK

skim

2% FAT

low

LOWEST FAT

FULL CREAM

Mapping Warm-up

This exercise will introduce Mind Mapping on a basic level and enable students to play with the nonlinear arrangement of ideas on paper before learning the specifics of Mind Mapping. A good Mind Mapping warm-up, this activity is also an excellent getting-to-know-you exercise.

Materials for Each Student:

- ✔ 10–12 circles or other shapes, cut from assorted colors of construction paper, in sizes from one to three inches. If you prefer, you can simply draw circles using a template on a master sheet (8 ½" x 11"), photocopy on colored sheets, and ask students to cut out their own.
- ✔ one sheet of unlined 11" x 17" paper
- ✔ crayons or colored water-based markers
- ✔ one glue stick

Select Shapes

Ask the students to select a circle that represents themselves and one circle for each person, place, or activity that is important in their lives. The size of the circles can be used to show relative importance to the student. For example, a child might select different sizes for self, Mom, Dad, sister, scouts, swimming lessons, school, baseball, friends, and a pet.

Place the Shapes

Have each child place the shapes on a large sheet of paper and move them around until their relative positions reflect the child's relationship to each aspect of his or her life. Ask children to look at the positions and decide if they are the right distance from each other.

Create the Map

Once the children are satisfied with the relative placement of the shapes, they should glue them in place. They can then use crayons and markers to draw lines, arrows, and other connecting marks between the circles. If children wish, they can draw images or symbols on the circles. As you can imagine, this exercise will give you insight into your students and help them see the larger picture of their lives.

Making Connections

Some children may be able to represent the strength of the relationships, the intensity of connections, and even mutuality. For example, if I have a friend with whom I have a balanced, reciprocal relationship, I might draw a thick line with arrow points on both ends. If I give more than I get in another relationship, I might show a one-way flow.

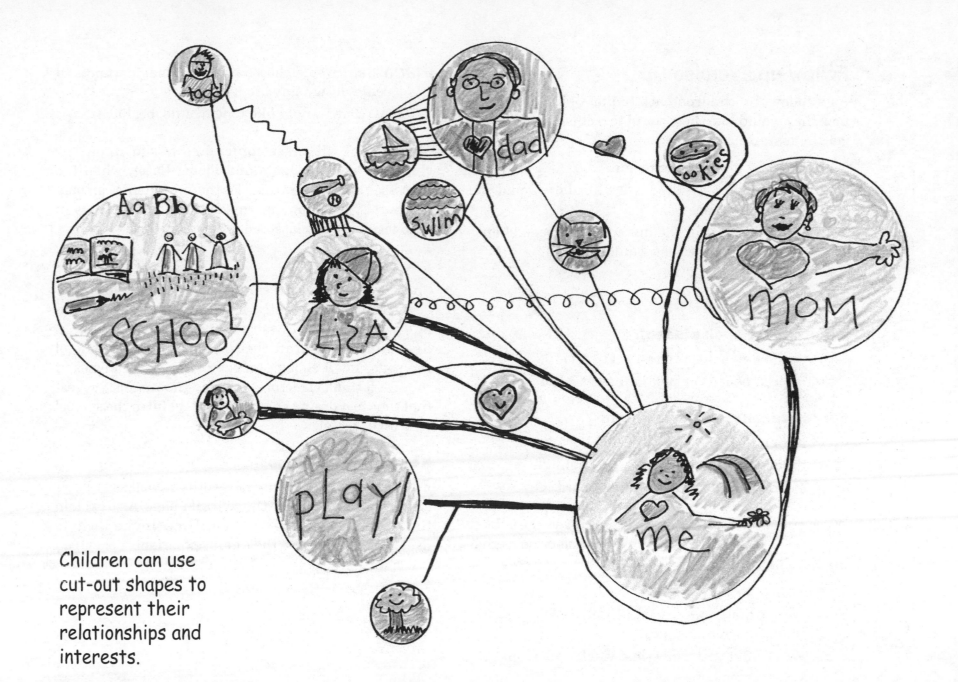

Children can use cut-out shapes to represent their relationships and interests.

Follow-up Exercise

As a follow-up, children each make a similar map of how they would like their world to be. Ask questions to get them started:

- What would you like to add?
- If you could have the perfect life, how would you place the shapes?
- What changes in the distances between shapes and their connections would be ideal?

Beginning Maps

Materials for each student:

- ✔ unlined paper (preferably 11" x 17")
- ✔ colored pencils or medium felt-tip markers

For the teacher demonstration:

- ✔ unlined paper, 26" x 33" (flip-chart size)
- ✔ broad-tip colored markers for highlighting
- ✔ colored chalk for use at chalkboard

When students are creating their first maps, the subject should be an easy one. Following are some topics that work well for first maps:

- Things I can do
- Who I am (my interests, goals, skills, friends, family, purpose, values)
- What I did yesterday (last week, this month)

- What I would choose if I had a magic wand and could design any life I wanted
- All that I would like to learn (do, be, have)

Notice that all these topics are based upon the children's own thoughts and ideas. Later, when the process is more comfortable for them, students can map topics they are studying in school and take notes in map form during classroom presentations.

Central Image

Show your students a simple Mind Map before they begin. Point out the central image. Ask children to begin by drawing a central symbol that represents their topic. Remind them to draw their symbol in the middle of the page, small enough to leave room for branches. If they can't think of pictures to begin their maps, suggest that they just draw a simple shape and fill in the symbol or drawing later.

Key Words and Symbols

Explain that they may use key words as well as symbols as they branch out from the central image. Also explain the value of using one word on a line. Invite them to use colors freely. (As they gain experience, they can use colors for coding and highlighting.)

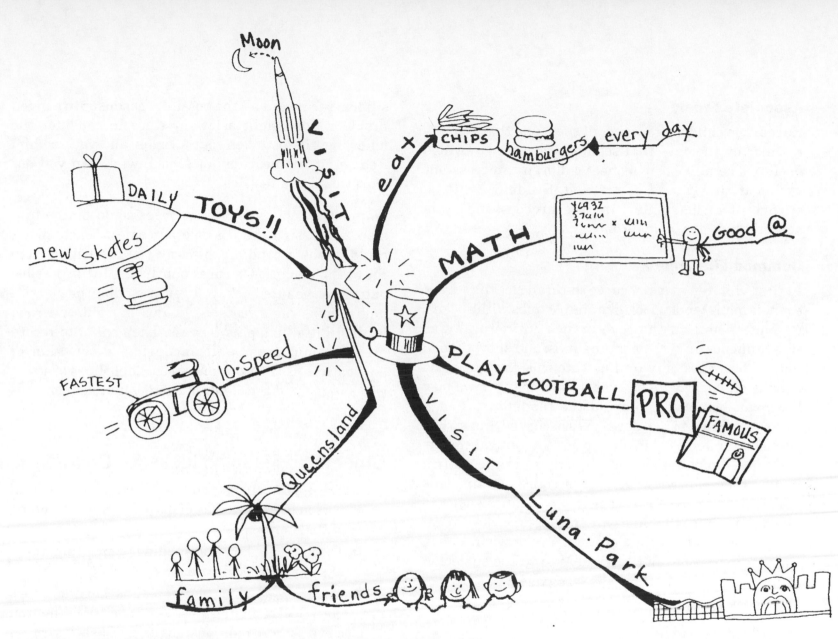

With a central image provided by the teacher, students branch off to record wishes. This visual map does not follow the Mind Map rule of one word per line, which is fine.

Associate Freely

Encourage children to write all the ideas that come to them, even the ones that seem far-fetched. Drawings need not be fancy or polished; children can cross out words if they make a mistake. Students will be surprised to learn that in this process, messy is acceptable, a new rule for most!

Common First-Map Problems

At first, children may not curve the branches they draw, so their maps tend to look like simple hubs with spokes. Remind them that they can branch out naturally, as tree branches grow from main limbs, and show them a map of branches only to illustrate this point (see the sample on page 25). The branch-only map shows how lines can be curved to avoid the tendency to write sideways and upside down. With curved lines that become thinner as they flow from the central image, and a "T" shape moving up directly from the central image, they can write all words right-side up. This makes the map easier to construct and much easier to read later. Notice that lines are thicker near the central image and taper as they grow. You may wish to give each learner a copy of the Mind Map on the subject of Mind Mapping from this book (see page 21).

Problem-Solving Map

You can demonstrate mapping to very young children using simple pictures. Children can create their own maps from age five on. You can use mapping with young students to record all the possible responses to a given problem. You might ask your class to consider the following: "If Joe takes your sweater and you see him wearing it the next day at school, what can you do? How would you feel?"

Mapping all the possible responses could be the first step. Discussing the possible outcome of each choice could be the second. In this way you branch off from the possible solution (such as punch him) to the possible outcomes (he hits back, you get in trouble, or he cries and returns the sweater). No idea is right or wrong in this initial mapping process. The goal is to record all ideas on paper and encourage discussion of alternatives. Ultimately, a few reasonable lines of action will emerge and the children can evaluate which ones they believe are the best ideas.

Other Mind Mapping Ideas for Children

- Tell a story to the children and then ask each person to create a map of his or her understanding of the story.
- Teach vocabulary and spelling by printing words next to symbols on a map.
- Use maps to show relationships, such as cause and effect or similarities. (See page 101.) Children can use these relationships as the basis of written sentences, such as "If _____ happens, then _____." Or "_____ and _____ are the same."

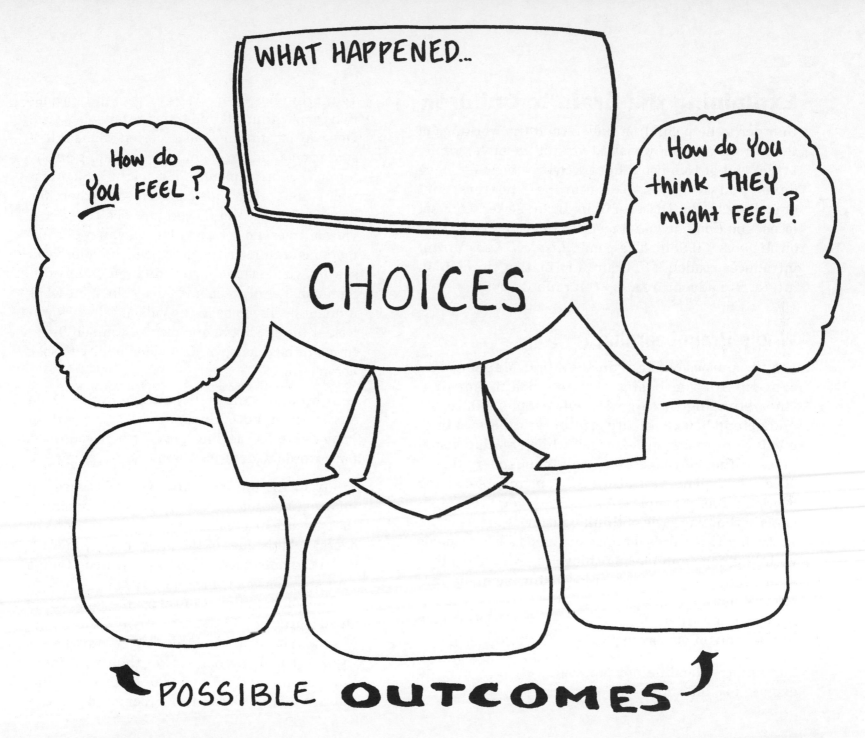

Explaining the Brain to Children

In order to help children understand the workings of their brains, you may wish to consult the bibliography at the end of this book. Robert Sylwester and I have developed two sets of audiotapes, posters, and guidebooks—the Discover Your Brain series. One set focuses on *Emotion and Attention* (1998a) and the other on *Memory* (1998b). The comic *Inside Brian's Brain* introduces students to brain information through an interactive adventure story (Margulies 1996).

Whole-Brain Learning

For the purpose of introducing Mind Mapping, you can explain the basics of whole-brain learning. Understanding these basics will enable children to understand how the creative, intuitive aspects of their mental processing are engaged while creating visual maps. Although the left and right hemisphere theory is easy to explain, it is also easily misunderstood and oversimplifies a complex process. Therefore, you might explain that one style of thinking is more active when we are writing words on lines because this style deals with language and placing things in order. The other style is more Mind Map–like, using symbols and colorful pictures, and creating new ideas that are not in any special order. Mapping and writing together help us use more of our brain power.

To reinforce the different processing styles, you could explain to children:

Your brain has many ways to take in information from within you and from the outside world. One way of thinking and experiencing is full of sensation and images. Imagine standing on the top of a beautiful mountain. Feel the air against your skin . . . hear music played somewhere far away . . . smell the flowers . . . see the whole view of trees, flowers, a village, a valley . . . and more mountains in the distance. The colors you see are wonderful . . . beautiful blues, many different shades of green and purple. Imagine what it might be like to be in the village below, as you look at the sky above and picture yourself flying through the clouds with a sudden ability to soar above it all.

Your brain has the ability to take in the whole picture, to dream of things you can't see but can imagine, to feel feelings, even when you don't have words to describe them.

"Your brain has another way of taking in information that you can think of by imagining that you are in a big building. There are rows of doors on both sides of the hallway. As you walk down the hall, you can go into any door. Count your steps as you walk along, 1, 2, 3, 4. Then go into a room and find it full of big file cabinets . . . Open a drawer and there, neatly filed, is a page of typewritten information. You read what it says . . . Open another drawer that has folders that are numbered 1 to 1,000! Notice, too, that there is a large clock in this room and you can

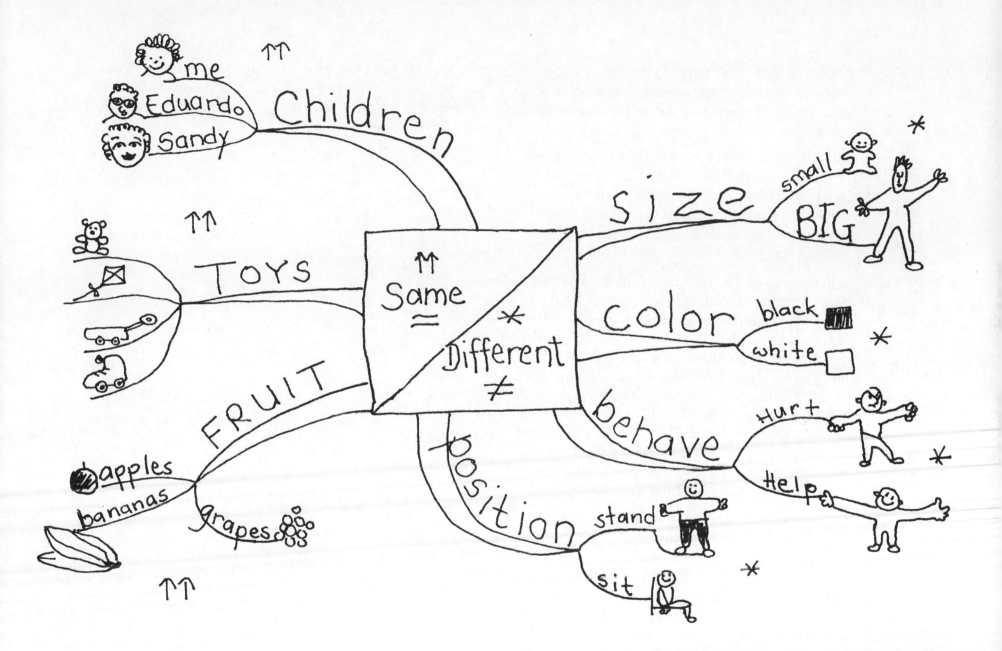

me
Eduardo
Sandy
⇈ Children

⇈ Toys

FRUIT
apples
bananas
grapes
⇈

Same
=
⇈
*
Different
≠

size
small
BIG *

color
black *
white *

behave
Hurt
Help *

position
stand
sit *

hear it ticking. This part of your brain learns in an orderly 1-2-3 way: the part that helps you keep track of time and pay attention to your teacher!

Luckily, we all have brains that can do many things: keeping our heart beating while imagining, feeling a range of emotions and sensations, adding numbers, being alert to danger, remembering songs, writing poems, playing soccer, and following the rules.

When you want to think of ideas for writing a paper, you need your whole brain to help you think of good ideas and put them in order. Mind Mapping appeals to the creative parts of you by using color, large sheets of paper, pictures, and no special order. This allows your imagination to flow. Later, you can use more logical 1-2-3 thinking skills to decide which ideas are best and put them in order. That way, you use your brain to think up lots of good ideas and see the connections among them, then decide which ideas are best and put them in order.

By using color and pictures, Mind Mapping makes remembering easier, too. If I ask you to think of the last chapter you studied in your social studies book, or the last library book you read, most of you think of a picture—maybe the cover of the book or an illustration. Not many people think of a sentence or paragraph of the book. Pictures are a big part of memory, so Mind Maps are easy to remember.

One thing you don't have to tell your young students is that mapping is fun—it is a natural way for them to express themselves and is wide open for personal variations and creativity.

Our brains process information in linear and global ways.

Chapter 5

Mapping with Older Students and Adults

You can introduce older students or adult groups to Mind Mapping by challenging them with the notion that our usual methods of note taking and writing papers don't work very well. Begin by asking them to list all the difficulties involved in writing one's own ideas on paper, or the problems of recording the ideas of others during meetings or lectures. The group will probably generate ideas such as the following common problems:

- It's hard to begin, so I postpone writing papers until the last minute.

- It is difficult to think of ideas in the right order.

- The process is often painfully slow and boring.

- It's hard to begin with a sense of the whole.

- It's difficult to listen and record ideas at the same time.

- My notes don't help me remember the material.

- There is no way to fit in new ideas where they belong in the notes.

After listing the limitations of traditional note taking, suggest that the group see these drawbacks as challenges in disguise. For example, the problem "it's hard to begin" could become the challenge: How can we create a system that is fun and makes it easy to get the writing process started? This new system would need to be fast, easy, and memorable. The entire group might then brainstorm a new system, or you might divide them into cooperative learning teams of three or four. Each team invents its own style of recording ideas and makes a sample of the system to show the others. As in all cooperative learning activities, each person in the team should be able to explain the new system as well as why and how it was created.

I have found that when the group combines the best of each new system, they come up with something that is surprisingly similar to Mind Mapping. You can then show the group examples of Mind Maps and other variations of visual mapping.

First Maps for Older Students and Adults

Learners can use mapping for purposes other than note taking. Mapping improves their study skills and expands their thinking capacity. They can also use mapping to brainstorm, review a complex curriculum, see patterns and relationships among ideas, and understand and apply complex concepts. (See chapters 1 and 2 for more mapping applications and examples.)

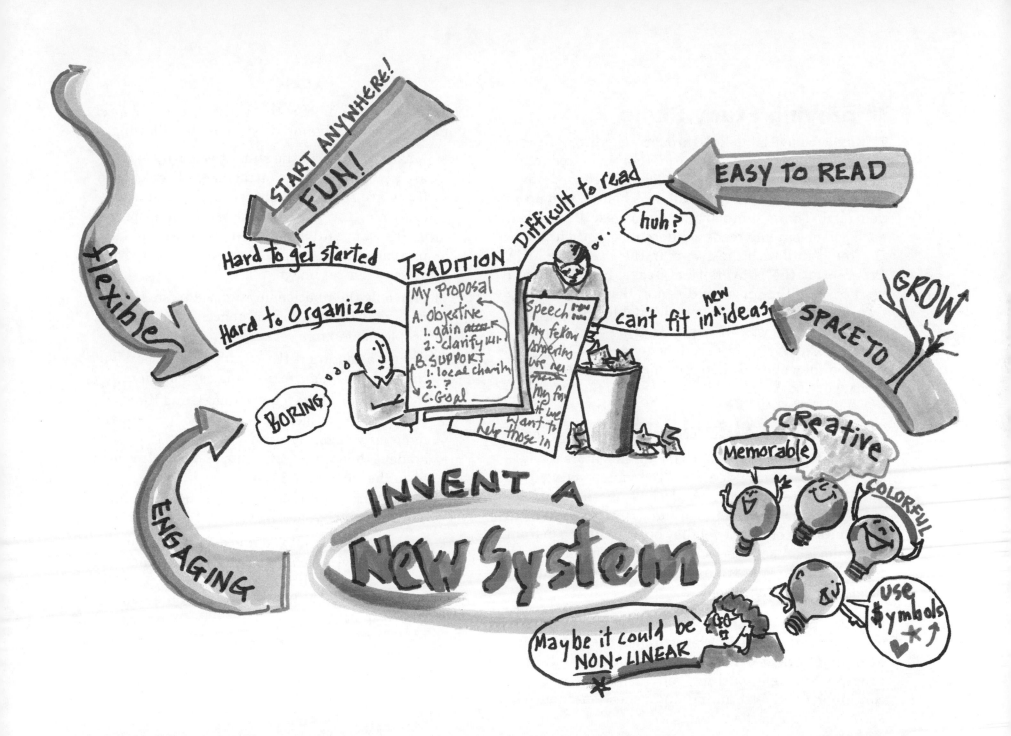

Improving Study Skills

It is often beneficial to look through an entire book, and map key parts before reading it. (For an introduction to this process, see page 38.) In addition to mapping a book *before* reading it in detail, it is helpful to map *as* you read. These summary maps are excellent when each person or team reads a different book, then shares the key points with the group. In the Executive MBA Program at the University of Texas, San Antonio, I worked with the program director, Bob Lengel, using this mapping approach, which enabled students to benefit from a host of books by sharing the key points in map form. Not every student read every book, but because they shared their insights, everyone learned from every book.

Activating Thinking Skills

One of the greatest problems facing educators today is that of the passive learner. Television as well as traditional teaching methods have both created a tendency in some students to sit back in the classroom with the same energy level they bring to sitting in front of a television set. The same is true of many adults who find themselves daydreaming during lengthy meetings or presentations.

Creating notes in Mind Map form requires more than writing down selected phrases from a book or lecture. Mapping reflects the learner's understanding of concepts and relationships and, at its best, requires continuous active thinking and reflection about the subject being recorded.

I recommend you enhance this active-learning aspect of mapping with assignments such as the following:

- Make two maps of the subject you are studying, each with a different central image. For example, if you are studying a short story in a literature class, map the story with the focus on a specific character, and then map it again with a particular setting, mood, theme, action, or event as your central image.

- Map only the relationships in a story or subject. For example, map the influences and impact on people related to a certain historical event.

- Create a map and then walk another student through your map, explaining each element.

- Read a story, make a map from it, and then give your map to another student, without telling the name of your story or discussing it. The other student then reads your map and from it writes his or her idea of the story.

- Map plans for a field trip. After the trip, map what actually occurred.

- Map situations that you find difficult to manage, such as moving to a new school or dealing with the presence of drugs or alcohol at a party. In small groups, add coping strategies to the maps as you share ideas.

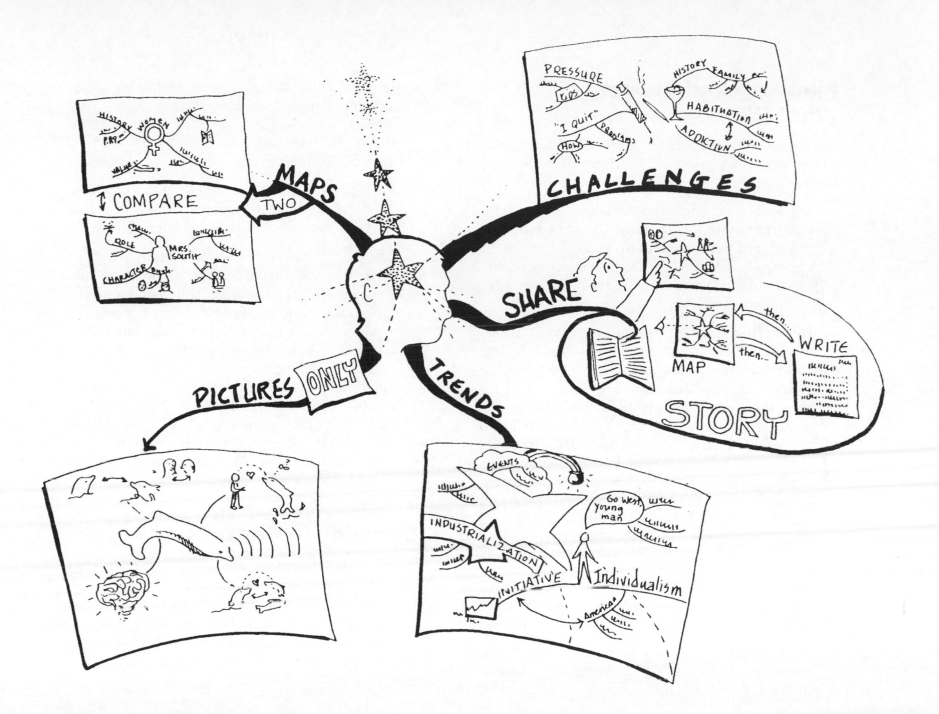

Mapping and Sharing What We Learn

Pat Dalton, when teaching high school science in St. Louis, Missouri, used Mind Maps with her biology classes and comments on her first experience:

> I wasn't very sophisticated about it—in fact I had just learned to map the day before I introduced the concept to my classes, but it went very well. I teach three classes in a row on the same subject, which is true for many teachers at my school.
>
> In the first class I introduced the basic terms we would be using as we studied animal classifications. I told the group we were going to try a new system—Mind Mapping—and for that we would need symbols. I asked them to work with me to develop little drawings to represent such categories as SOFT-BODIED CREATURES and MOLLUSKS. We had fun coming up with ideas. I especially liked the fish and person in a file drawer to represent the fact that humans and fish are in the same phylum. These mnemonic devices really helped the students recall the terms.
>
> Once we had our basic symbols on the board, everyone copied them, and we had a map of biological classifications.
>
> The next group came in and, rather than erasing the board and beginning all over again, I decided to show them the symbols the class before them had just created. In doing so, I explained each classification, and we moved on from there. That second-hour class got further in the material than the first and had time to invent new symbols for the next lesson.
>
> The third class had the benefit of the first two, moved along rapidly through the material, and made up symbols for the last section of the unit.
>
> The next day I showed the first group what the other two had invented, and we were off and running. Now the benefit of this, aside from the fact that it was fun, is that when I tested my students on the material, I was amazed at how much they remembered. I tried traditional tests on the first two groups, and then for my third-hour class, I used Mind Mapping as a part of the test. To accomplish that, I showed them a map I had made of the symbols and asked them to select two branches of the map and write an essay about them. Again, the recall of the material was very impressive.

Learning in Context

In school settings, as at home, one of the challenges of teaching is conveying the *context* as well as the concept. For example, learning a fact of history may seem meaningless and hard to remember unless you understand it in the larger context of historical trends, cause and effect, and its potential relationship to current events.

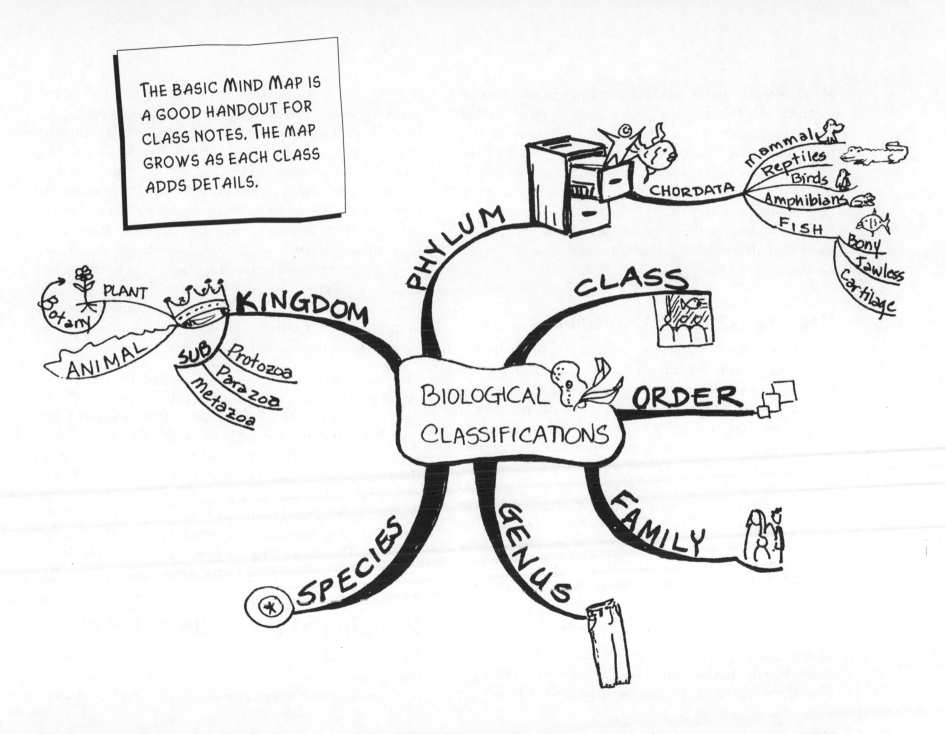

THE BASIC MIND MAP IS A GOOD HANDOUT FOR CLASS NOTES. THE MAP GROWS AS EACH CLASS ADDS DETAILS.

PHYLUM

CHORDATA
mammal
Reptiles
Birds
Amphibians
FISH
Bony
Jawless
Cartilage

CLASS

PLANT
Botany
ANIMAL
KINGDOM
SUB
Protozoa
Parazoa
Metazoa

BIOLOGICAL CLASSIFICATIONS

ORDER

FAMILY

GENUS

SPECIES

Memory works best when you can understand new information in relationship to existing information. For example, when you hear or read a fact about a country that you know little or nothing about, you have no memory anchor for this new information and are likely to forget it quickly. Quite the opposite occurs when you hear about a country that you've visited. You are more likely to remember the information because you already have a wealth of associations, memories, and impressions about that country.

Mapping a Complex Curriculum

Let's look at one teacher, one lesson plan, to see how to apply mapping to a complex curriculum from start to finish. I have selected a unit developed by a master educator who brings the arts into any subject matter he teaches. Alan Warhaftig teaches American literature to 11th graders in Los Angeles. His students come from diverse backgrounds and represent a variety of learning styles and skill levels. The book that they read and discuss is one that is brilliant, intricate, and challenging: *Invisible Man* by Ralph Ellison. Woven within the complex plot are allusions to the history, politics, and culture of the early and mid-20th century, as well as a theme that is close to the heart of high school students: personal identity and the search for a sense of belonging.

In order to immerse his students fully in the life and times in which the nameless narrator, the invisible man, lives, Warhaftig introduces his class to the history, music, poetry, artifacts, and paintings that link to Ellison's novel. His students can then approach the reading with a sense of context. They learn about the role the arts play in defining and reflecting an era. In fact, they are immersed in that world as they probe deeply into the book. He explains, "Thinking in musical terms also helps students improve their writing. Words correspond to the notes and punctuation to the rests. Like music, writing can have a rhythm; it can be harmonious or it can be jarring." Listening to music in class can calm students or energize them as well as broaden their perspectives. (For more information about this curriculum, contact Mr. Warhaftig at Warhaftig@alumni.stanford.org.)

The visual map on the opposite page records topics for maps that students could create to represent their understanding of the book. Due to the complexity of the novel, students should begin with just a few topics in mind so that they can read with an eye to those themes. As they read, they can fill in their maps. They can build individual maps, work with a partner, or create a group mural map recording the various themes and layers of meaning. It is often helpful to map questions that come up while reading, or incidents from one's life that are similar to the story.

Mapping at the College Level

Bernice Bleedorn, the Director for Creative Studies at the College of St. Thomas in St. Paul, Minnesota, has been using Mind Mapping with college students since

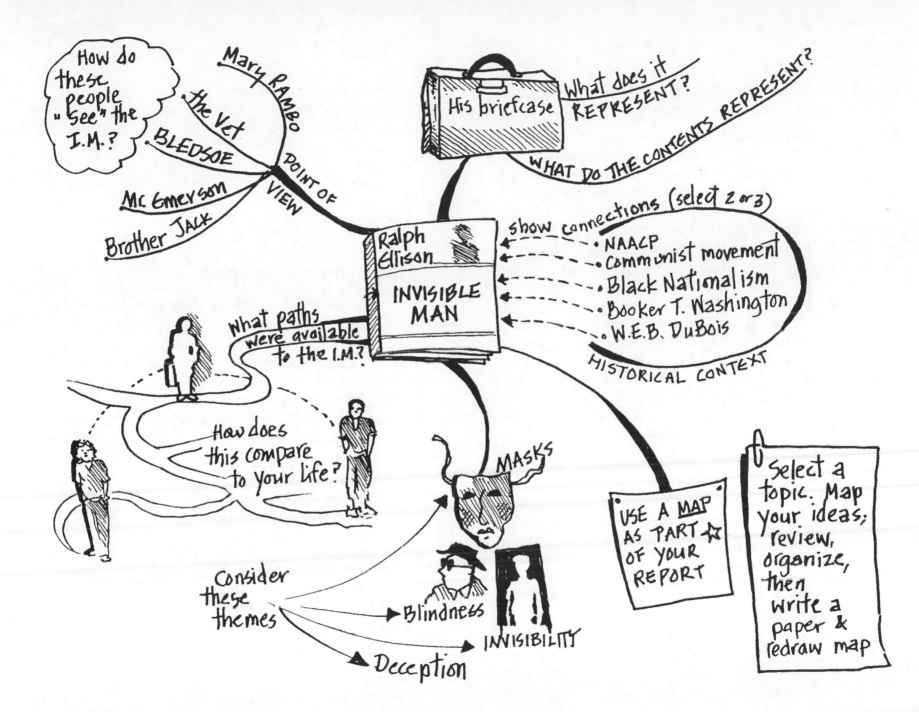

How do these people "see" the I.M.?

Mary RAMBO
the Vet
BLEDSOE
Mc Emerson
Brother JACK

POINT OF VIEW

His briefcase — What does it REPRESENT?
WHAT DO THE CONTENTS REPRESENT?

Ralph Ellison
INVISIBLE MAN

show connections (select 2 or 3)
• NAACP
• Communist movement
• Black Nationalism
• Booker T. Washington
• W.E.B. DuBois

HISTORICAL CONTEXT

What paths were available to the I.M.?

How does this compare to your life?

MASKS

Consider these themes
Blindness
INVISIBILITY
Deception

USE A MAP AS PART OF YOUR REPORT ☆

Select a topic. Map your ideas; review, organize, then write a paper & redraw map she first learned the technique in the early '80s. Her approach can be used with high school students as well.

I have made extensive use of mapping for generating ideas and planning the writing of papers and articles for publication, as well as planning talks and seminars. Mapping has become the 'first line of attack' for just about any substantial communication. More specifically, I am constantly promoting mapping in my classes. I require the presentation of a book review on a book relevant to the course content, chosen by the student, read, and mapped for the class. Maps are brought to class, and the presentations are made from the maps rather than from a complex set of notes or formal paper. I make a strong case for 'whole brain thinking,' with mapping an aid to balancing spontaneous, systematic, visual thinking and communicating with traditional sequential, verbal systems.

Mapping as a strategy has been transferring successfully to other educational settings. Teachers who have been in my creative studies class . . . report that when they introduce the concept of mapping and encourage it as an alternative language, students in elementary grades who have been relatively constrained in their writing assignments begin to express complex thinking patterns through the creation of a map. New thinking 'stars' are discovered when alternative communication systems are introduced.

Students from my undergraduate course on entrepreneurial creative thinking and problem solving develop some extremely effective maps; and book reviews presented from maps take on a particularly energetic and articulate style. It becomes clear that students have really internalized the reading material and understand it as a system.

Mapping Concepts

For many years, I have attended conferences, not only to teach Mind Mapping, but also to create visual maps while others present new information. These poster-size maps are displayed on the walls and serve as points for review and discussion. As a result of this work, I have met and worked with an amazing group of educators and business leaders. One of the most fascinating is Parker Palmer, an educator and theologian who is the author of many books, including *The Courage to Teach: Exploring the Inner Landscape of a Teacher's Life* (1997) and *To Know As We Are Known* (1993).

I created the map on the opposite page during one of Palmer's presentations to faculty and administrators from undergraduate programs throughout the country. The map serves as a sample to illustrate mapping concepts, but more important, the content touches upon some key issues facing educators today.

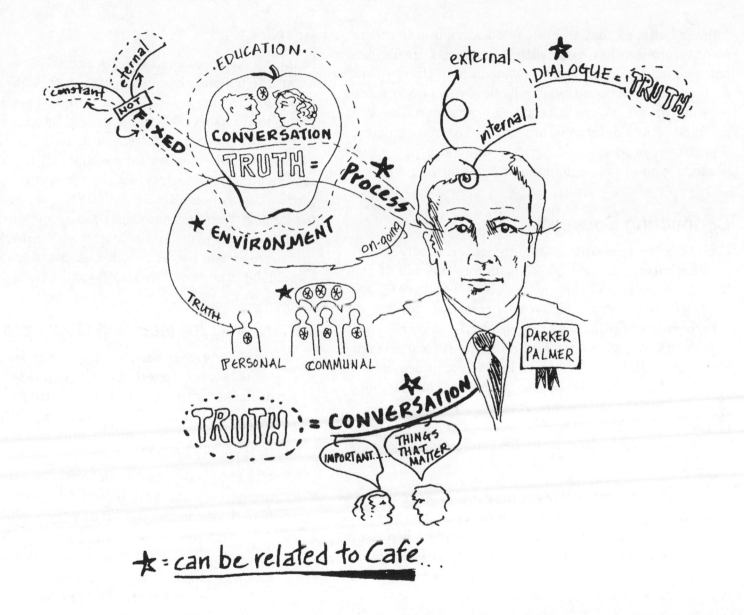

EDUCATION

external

DIALOGUE = TRUTH ⭐

eternal

constant

NOT FIXED

CONVERSATION

TRUTH =

⭐ Process

internal

on-going

⭐ ENVIRONMENT

TRUTH

⭐

PERSONAL   COMMUNAL

PARKER PALMER

TRUTH = CONVERSATION ⭐

IMPORTANT...   THINGS THAT MATTER

⭐ = can be related to Café...

Palmer believes that the role of education is to create an environment in which truth is practiced. He defines *truth* as an ongoing conversation about things that matter. This conversation can be between two or more persons, or it can be an internal conversation. There is no fixed, eternal, or constant truth, Palmer explains. Truth is a *process* and depends upon the person or persons who are experiencing and examining it.

Connecting Concepts

Considering the way in which we create truth in conversation leads me to think about the use of the World Café process (for more details about café, see page 40). Conversation is an important aspect of interpersonal skills. Assisting students to clarify and express their own needs and opinions (intrapersonal skills) as well as to "listen to learn" could occur in a café setting. I map these ideas on the Palmer map, placing a star by each element of his presentation that relates to the World Café. Eventually, I decide to create a new map that builds on the first map but focuses on the café process.

Remembering that the World Café centers on questions that matter, I brainstorm and map topics that would be of great interest to students. The topic I feel is of extreme interest is violence in schools, so I highlight that on the map. Branching from there, I list questions that might engage everyone in the café.

Act!

Mapping is an excellent way to record all my thoughts about the people who might support this effort to hold a café forum for students. Next I might prepare a map to use as an aspect of a presentation or enclosure with a letter to the organizations and individuals I have identified. This map would emphasize the benefits of café as a methodology, especially for students who can participate with adults as equals. When the group meets to plan logistics, such as location, date, and participants, I can map as the group brainstorms. While the café is in progress, someone can map as participants share their insights and new ideas on the topic of school violence.

Other Ideas for Mapping Concepts

- Challenge your class to map a design for a new school system based upon the equality principles of Parker Palmer and incorporating the process of the World Café. What would the schedule, class groupings, topics, and grading system look like in this new school?

- Use café activities to reinforce the conversation among students and to help them experience the benefit of sharing points of view.

- Ask students to map what they know about a given topic, such as violence in schools, then discuss their maps. While listening to the information and ideas of others, each person adds to his or her own map.

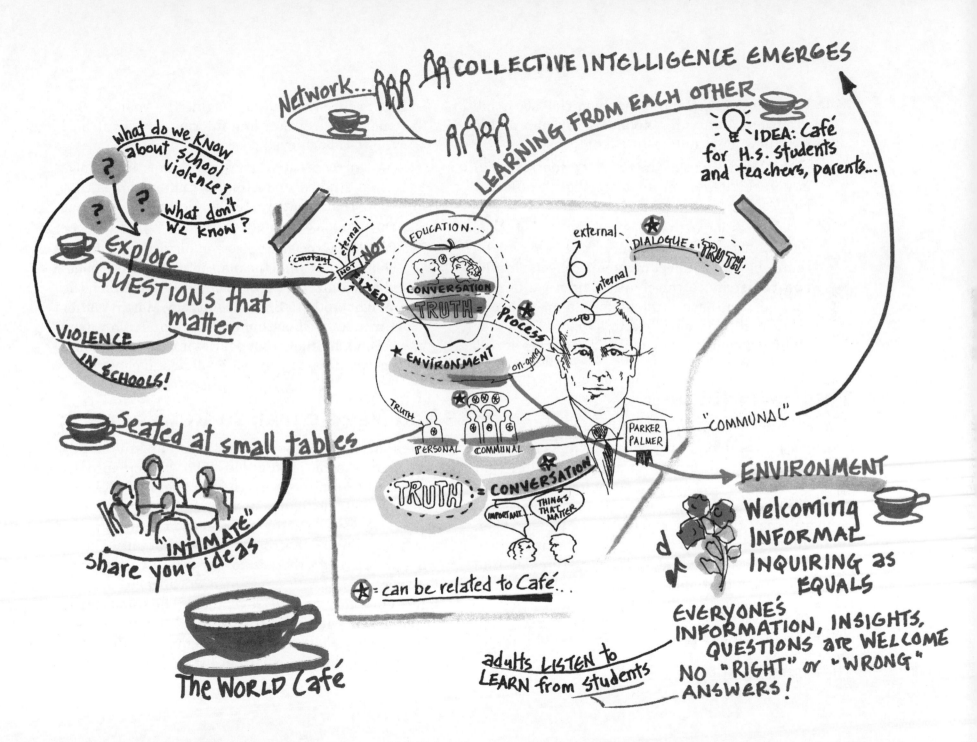

COLLECTIVE INTELLIGENCE EMERGES

Network...

LEARNING FROM EACH OTHER

IDEA: Café for H.S. Students and teachers, parents...

What do we KNOW about school violence?

What don't we know?

Explore QUESTIONS that matter

VIOLENCE IN SCHOOLS!

EDUCATION

external constant NOT FIXED

CONVERSATION TRUTH =

Process

ENVIRONMENT

on-going

external

internal

DIALOGUE = TRUTH

PARKER PALMER

"COMMUNAL"

Seated at small tables

TRUTH

PERSONAL   COMMUNAL

"INTIMATE"
Share your ideas

TRUTH = CONVERSATION

IMPORTANT...   THINGS THAT MATTER

ENVIRONMENT

Welcoming INFORMAL INQUIRING as EQUALS

⚝ = can be related to Café...

The WORLD Café

adults LISTEN to LEARN from students

EVERYONE'S INFORMATION, INSIGHTS, QUESTIONS are WELCOME
NO "RIGHT" or "WRONG" ANSWERS!

- Have students take their map on violence home to a friend and, while explaining the map, add to it all new ideas or questions that arise.
- Make Mind Maps on the topic of a controversial issue, asking everyone to take a slightly different point of view and map it.
- Pose a question to the class and ask each student to map his or her opinions in one color in the center of a large sheet of paper. Collect, shuffle, and redistribute the maps. Using a different colored pen, each student builds on someone else's map, adding ideas to support the other student's point of view, even if they don't agree!

The Outer Edge

In science, there is a concept called *edge of the map syndrome,* which refers to the belief scientists have had, at various times through the ages, that they had discovered all there was to know about a certain subject: They had reached the edge of the map, and there was no more. Each time they reached the edge, however, some foolhardy soul ventured off the map into unimagined territories and, naturally, stumbled into new information that made the old obsolete.

I like to borrow this concept when mapping. I often challenge students to place their completed map on a larger sheet of paper and go over the edge. Try the following ideas with your students.

- Ask your students to imagine the year is 2020 and they are recording information about how the world achieved peace.
- Assign cooperative learning groups in science, social studies, or history to find examples that show that what was once known as truth has since been completely revised.
- Challenge social studies and history students to create a map (like the map on the opposite page) of boundary breakers, such as Junko Tabei, the Wright brothers, Susan B. Anthony, Martin Luther King, and Christopher Columbus. The area beyond the known boundaries is rich with infinite possibilities, so why not explore and chart it?

You Need a Map to Get There!

To emphasize this point with younger students, I pretend to be some strange lady who wanders into the class asking for directions. "How do I get there?" I ask. "Can you help me figure out where to go to get there?" When they ask, "Where? Where do you want to go?" I say, "I don't know!" It becomes obvious that until I know where I want to go, there is no way to figure out how to get there. If I say, "I want to go to Chicago," we can figure out many ways to travel there. The same is true of life, and I encourage children and adults alike to make frequent maps to help them figure out where they want to go and what they want to be able to do, have, and be.

Chapter 6

Mapping in Business and Community Settings

This chapter introduces samples of a variety of mapping styles, all related to business and learning. The uses for mapping in these contexts include planning presentations, communicating new ideas, organizing projects, and looking at systems to gain insight into complex organizations and patterns of behavior.

Visual mapping is a full-time career for many men and women. This relatively new field is growing rapidly, as businesses and community groups see the value of the visual approach. In the Resources section of this book, you will find information about how to contact visual recorders (also called *visual* or *graphic facilitators*) and the names of seminars in which you can learn the skills required for this unique profession.

You can use any of the maps in this chapter as inspiration for maps you make yourself. Although your maps may not look like those of a professional visual recorder, the process will enable you to learn and to accomplish your work in an expedient, organized, and creative manner.

Mary Corrigan, a professional mapper, records and facilitates meetings all over the world. In her own words:

> It is a joy to make my living creating visual maps, working as a graphic recorder in business settings. When I started in this work, I didn't think I could draw and had no artistic training. What compelled (or I should say propelled) me into learning to map was the incredible creative opportunity I saw to bring a new life to group work. Seeing ideas mapped enables groups to learn and think together.
>
> Enabling others to see their own ideas recorded in this manner fits with my deep desire to be part of a community that helps people learn, communicate, and work more effectively together. I was completely taken by the power with which visual images can move people forward together. As I continue to work in this field, my ability to listen deeply and notice the connections among ideas continues to develop.

Learning Reviews

The learning review is a powerful process. Originally developed by the United States Army as "after action reviews," the review's purpose is to generate learning

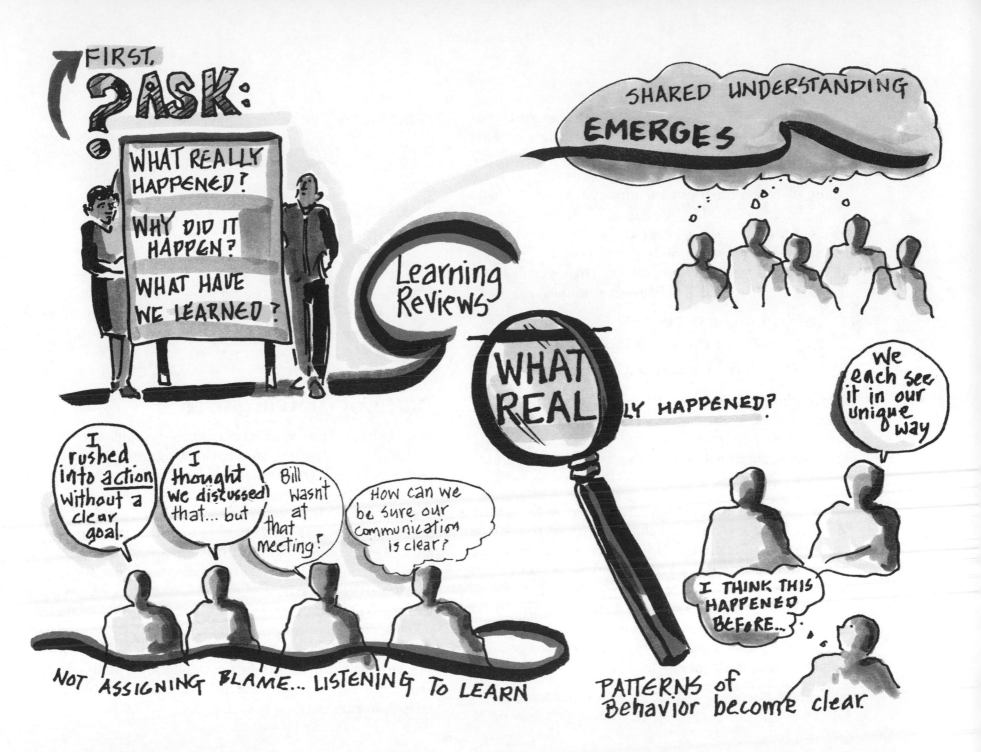

during and after battle. This process has been adapted for use in business and educational settings by Meg Wheatley and Myron Kellner-Rogers. Myron has further developed the process in partnership with his clients. Work carried out in conjunction with Unocal Corporation, with Mary Corrigan as visual recorder, has enabled groups of employees in a number of different countries to review and learn from their experiences. Those who were involved in a specific event meet as equals to focus on three questions:

1. **What really happened?**
2. **Why do we think it happened?**
3. **What have we learned?**

As the group explores each question, the diversity of points of view enables a richer understanding of what occurred and helps to clear up misunderstandings. Without assigning blame, the participants evaluate their own participation.

Mary records the collective learning of the group visually so everyone can relate and react to it. This enables the participants to engage in an open and honest conversation about the difficult issues they must address in order to learn from their experiences. Patterns of behavior and interaction become clear. Learning takes place not because any one person is teaching, but because the group is open to gaining valuable insights from one another.

Next Steps

After identifying the patterns of behavior, the structures, and the processes involved in the event, the group asks more questions:

1. **What do we abandon?**
2. **What do we keep?**
3. **What do we create?**

It is a powerful experience when a group comes to a shared view of what needs to change (or continue as is) to achieve the desired level of performance in their future work.

Cultural Convergence

Nusa has developed another way to use visual mapping to facilitate deeper understanding and shared perspective in a group. After working with a number of companies that had split into separate business units, or were involved in new joint ventures, she observed that two groups coming together sometimes clicked, with open communication and new plans flowing like improvisational music. When they didn't click, disappointments and misunderstandings arose, leading key people to become less involved. Team members would comply rather than commit to a shared purpose. Many rules in any business are not "official"— they are tacit understandings that not everyone shares or recognizes. Maps can clarify and communicate the unspoken rules so that everyone is aware of them.

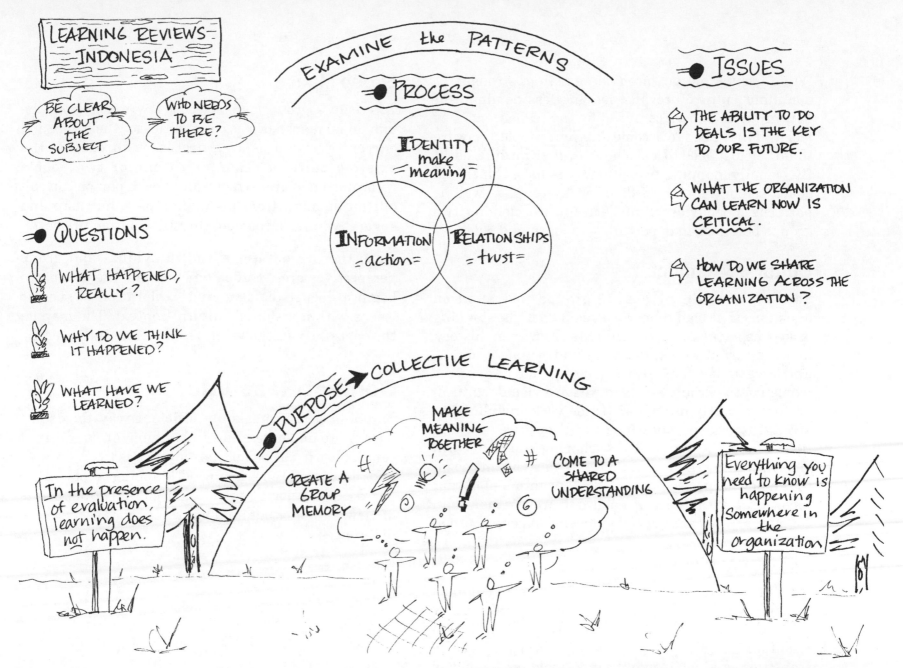

LEARNING REVIEWS — INDONESIA

BE CLEAR ABOUT THE SUBJECT

WHO NEEDS TO BE THERE?

EXAMINE the PATTERNS

● PROCESS

IDENTITY = make meaning =

INFORMATION = action =

RELATIONSHIPS = trust =

● QUESTIONS

WHAT HAPPENED, REALLY?

WHY DO WE THINK IT HAPPENED?

WHAT HAVE WE LEARNED?

● ISSUES

THE ABILITY TO DO DEALS IS THE KEY TO OUR FUTURE.

WHAT THE ORGANIZATION CAN LEARN NOW IS CRITICAL.

HOW DO WE SHARE LEARNING ACROSS THE ORGANIZATION?

● PURPOSE ➔ COLLECTIVE LEARNING

MAKE MEANING TOGETHER

CREATE A GROUP MEMORY

COME TO A SHARED UNDERSTANDING

In the presence of evaluation, learning does not happen.

Everything you need to know is happening somewhere in the organization

This visual map was created by Mary Corrigan during a learning review. (Used with permission.)

When groups merge, often the existing, stronger, or dominant culture prevails, leaving less dominant or new group members confused by the transition. They feel as if they need to become different people, unaware that they just need to learn how to *navigate* differently. By visually mapping transition dynamics, values and goals, strengths and needs of each group, as well as patterns of behavior within each culture, blending two groups becomes an opportunity to learn and evolve.

Cultural Architecture

You might begin by asking groups in transition questions that lead them to develop an understanding of key aspects such as highlights from their history, how they usually make decisions and evaluate success, and strategies for the future. As you map these elements, the group begins to weave a visual "cultural architecture." This visual framework includes the strengths and perspectives of all cultures coming together in the group. By anchoring these cultural elements with graphics on the walls, participants begin to see how to put the pieces together into a plan that incorporates the best of each culture. Rather than competing, they are invited to learn from one another.

Individual Maps

After the groups share cultural elements, individuals can map their own explorations of questions about new roles and responsibilities, their ideal roles and contributions in the new organization, concerns about the transition, and what might be possible for the newly forming group.

Group Map

To create a group map, select a few topics from the individual maps, such as possibilities for the future and current decision-making processes in each of the existing cultures. Then, with one or two people recording on a large paper mural, each person can call out an element from his or her personal map and suggest where on the map this information fits best.

Once the presentations and individual and group perspectives are recorded on one map, the group can begin a deeper dialogue and exploration of specific issues within a shared cultural context. The map on the opposite page shows the result of one such process.

Conflict Resolution

Mapping is a remarkably efficient way to resolve barriers to understanding and alignment. The crux of conflict lies in the belief that "my way is the right way, and there is only one right way." Mapping reveals other perspectives, moving the focus from individual points of view and creating an opportunity for resolution of differences.

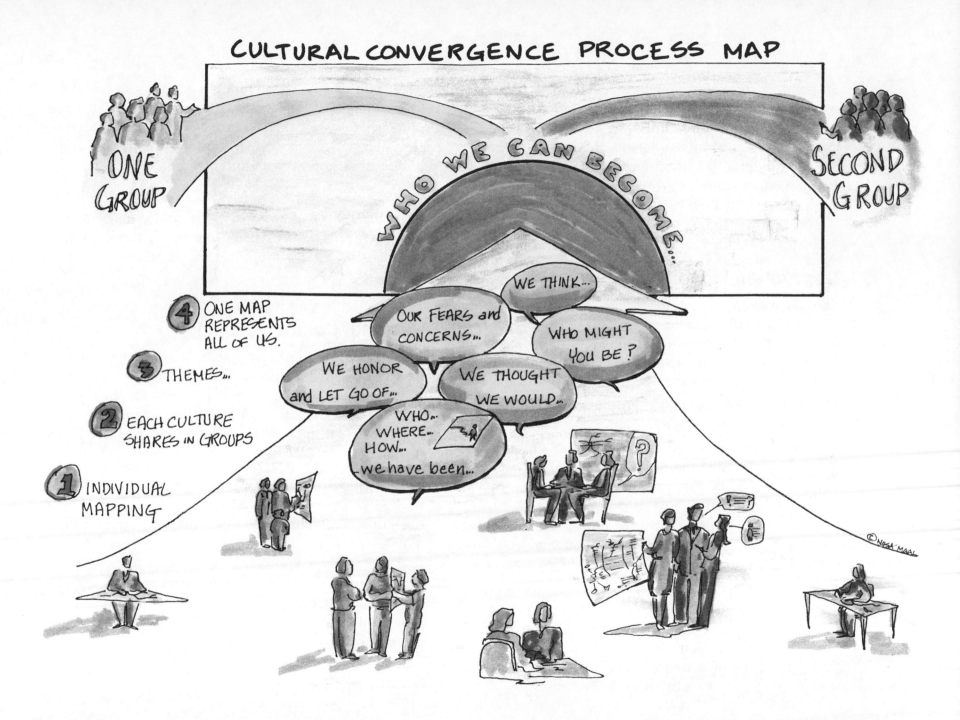

Stephen Covey recommends we "seek first to understand" (1990). Mapping helps create a safe listening and sharing environment in which the focus is on the visual representations and ideas of others rather than on the individual points of contention. Taking the sting out of conflict, and creating a more objective forum, mapping quickly facilitates a deeper understanding of issues.

Negotiation Mapping

The following approach to conflict resolution has been used in union/management negotiations as well as for conflict resolution within teams. Provide sheets of 11" x 17" paper and several colored felt-tip pens for each participant. Ask each person to take these steps:

1. Draw a symbol of a successful resolution in the center of your sheet of paper.
2. Next, on branches connecting to the center, record the details of the ideal outcome of this conflict (negotiation, issue). Use a different branch for each aspect.
3. Selecting a different color, add to each branch a line on which you record what you would be willing to do to further the ideal outcome.

The group is then paired up so that one person from each side of the argument is partnered with someone from the opposing group. A union woman may be partnered with a man from management. A member of a group in favor of a merger may be partnered with someone who opposes the idea.

Each pair is given the same assignment: Create a shared map that reflects only the areas where you agree and includes what either one of you would do to further that end. Don't worry about differences at this time; just look for and map similarities.

The outcome of such a process is that the focus shifts from differences to areas of agreement, and members from opposing sides experience working together on a common task. A more productive discussion can then ensue.

Personal Conflict Mapping

In another variation of mapping, each person (or group) creates a Mind Map illustrating his or her position in a conflict. Participants include a branch for the hurtful incident(s), and another for how they felt and feel. They also include branches for expectations, requests, and disappointments.

Because pictures tell more than words, mapping opens pathways to emotional empathy. In one long-term dispute, when feuding coworkers mapped their conflict, barriers came down, opening communication between them as they recognized the emotional impact of the dispute and connected on a more personal level. After listening and sharing maps, each of the parties saw the world from the perspective of the other, in a larger context, making resolution more likely.

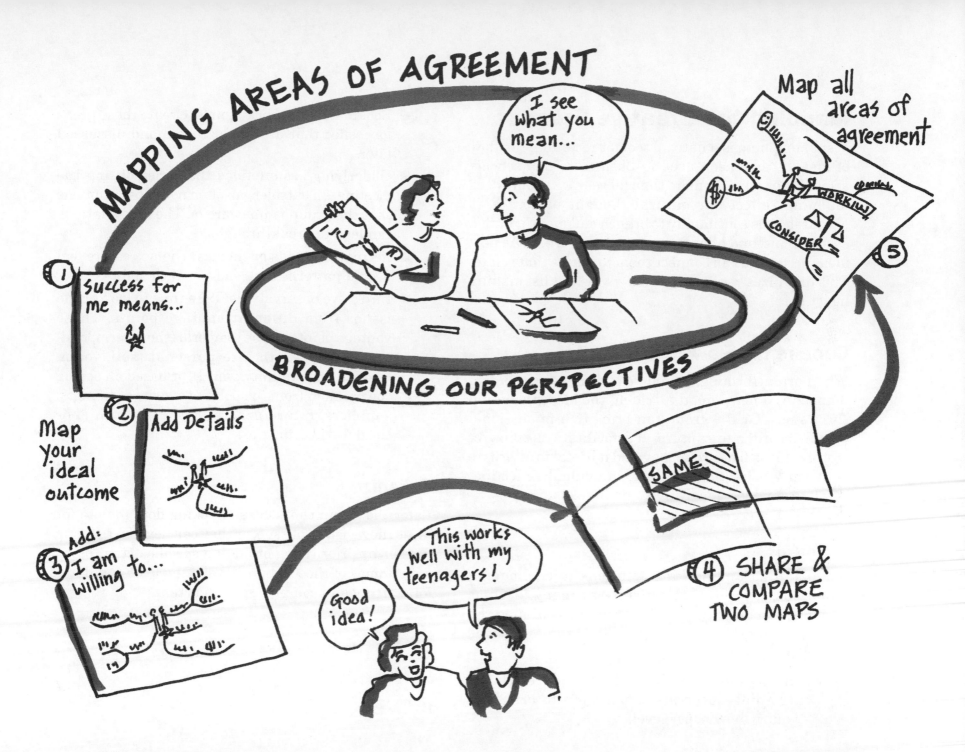

Mapping the Creative Process

Visual mapping is a natural tool for recording the flow of ideas. It has been used in businesses and schools around the world for more than 20 years. Not only does mapping reflect our natural thought processes, it encourages us continually to branch out, make creative associations, and allow our ideas to flow freely. As new ideas occur, you can connect them to others that relate. This organizes your thoughts in a way that list making never can.

Capture the Flow

When brainstorming, a group can designate a central mapper or a map-squad to "catch" the ideas the group throws out. Or the group can bring in a professional visual recorder to capture and facilitate the flow of creative ideas. The group may find it useful to alternate between whole-group process, individual reflection, small-group idea generation, and breaks.

Generate

For planning and seeking solutions to challenging situations, it is ideal to generate as many ideas as possible. You may wish to place flip charts around the room to record various aspects of the process, such as the following:

- All the questions that arise, to address later: Recording questions enables you to bring the inquiry to a deeper level.

- Bookmarks and parking lots: Create these areas for issues that are better tabled and discussed later.
- Underlying assumptions that arise during the meeting: An outsider can often notice assumptions that the group is unaware of. These revelations can lead to breakthroughs.
- Recurrent trends or themes: Themes can reveal deeper patterns and lead to new insights.
- Bird's-eye observations: Take time to look at the issues from different vantage points. These vantage points can be temporal (short-term, mid-term, long-term), interpersonal (self, team, company, community, world), or based on seeing the problem from the point of view of customers, suppliers, future generations, competitors, or third world countries.

Organize

Later the group can use self-sticking dots to vote for ideas they wish to pursue, or they can develop the map further by prioritizing or adding specific action plans with names of those who will take the lead and dates for starting and completing each action.

Clarifying Purpose

Asking "What drew you to this work or organization?" or "Why are we here?" often rekindles a passion for the work. People may work together with different ideas of the company's purpose, using the same words yet meaning something very different. Asking the question and visually mapping the responses and relationships can surface differences, as well as surfacing shared passions.

For example, a small group of leaders of a multilateral organization gathered for a strategic planning session. They shared a clear idea of why they were seeking effective strategies to unify global nutrition efforts and understanding. They had evidence that if successful with their vision, every newborn child could be adequately nourished through infancy in our lifetime.

However, they were disconnected from their original motivating passion. After discussion and review of the maps, they dedicated a large chart to the question: "Why are we really here?" From this they arrived at profound insights.

The leader of this program felt exhausted by the magnitude of the challenge and limited resources. She and the organization had begun to feel as powerless as the people they represented.

This phenomenon occurs all the time with children as well as adults—with physical as well as emotional pain based on feeling powerless or overwhelmed. Because they were able to understand this pattern in context, when the group finished, they shared a clear understanding of the way feeling powerless could derail their efforts. They then were able to look beyond emotions and ascertain the role of important players in their field. Once the players were identified, the power dynamics became easier to identify. As they developed a strategy with contingencies, their leader felt reconnected with her deep passion for her work, and all were encouraged by their expanded perspective and team cohesion.

In this way, visual mapping not only helps us see the steps we want to take to achieve our aims, it also helps us understand the way we step, and why.

Team Presentations

A facilitator can use visual mapping as a productive and efficient way to bring teams together, build presentation skills, and provide user-friendly graphics at the same time. By visually mapping key questions about the project, graphic facilitators help teams see the parts and the whole context of their situation and make the most of their individual styles and areas of expertise. This process enables them to determine which information is pertinent for their desired outcome. It helps them to identify quickly the heart of their concerns. From there, they can more efficiently choose roles.

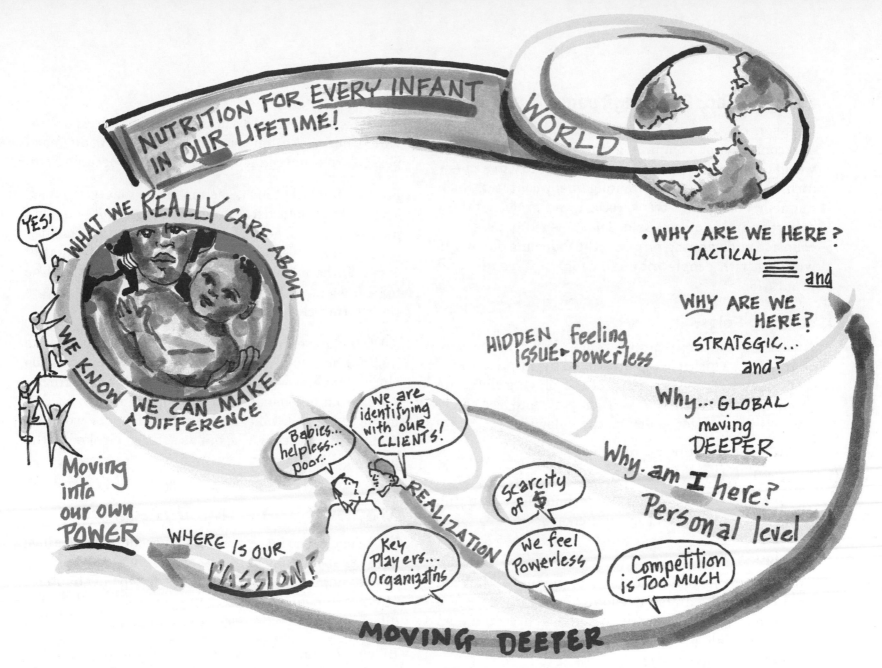

Using visual mapping to reveal hidden barriers and clarify the shared vision of an organization. (Used with permission.)

Sample Map: Bringing Teams Together

Members of a team from a top commercial management and construction company gathered from all over the world to prepare a presentation, hoping to win a major airline construction and management contract. Each member had a long track record and great depth of expertise in his or her field. They needed to present a cohesive and winning proposal the following day, while working with people they knew only by resume and reputation.

Mapping Roles

Nusa recorded their multileveled discussion on flip-chart paper, which was set up around the meeting room. Once they had a clear sense of the playing field, the group explored their role as a company and as a team, addressing questions such as the following:

- What might be required of us later?
- What do we have to offer?
- What specific experiences and corresponding lessons make us the right choice?

Ambiguity Map

They also dedicated a map to all of the things they did not know. As the ambiguity map quickly filled up, the individuals became more calm and able to craft a plan that included an understanding that unknown variables were part of the picture.

Review

Each person reviewed the maps, marking areas for which he or she felt responsible. As a result, each person's role and connection to the whole became clear.

For the finishing touch, each member met with Nusa. The sessions yielded a set of flip-chart graphics for team members to use to anchor their key points as they presented the essence of their proposal to the potential client. Without looking at any other notes, they felt free to be present with authenticity and responsiveness to their future client.

After the presentation, the eldest team member—who insisted he had always used linear notes and was too old to change—was very excited: "It was amazing! I spoke from my visuals and I never even went back to my notes at the table. I was worried that I wouldn't remember all the details, but as soon as I looked at the pictures, I remembered everything."

Mapping Meeting Dynamics

Most people who have spent their workdays in meetings agree that meetings often seem like a waste of time. Visual mapping following the basic steps in chapter 1 offers a fun and efficient framework to solve this dilemma.

By clearly mapping the purpose of the meeting, the group can focus the conversation on a shared sense of agreement. Thus prepared, the group can freely express

These visual maps unified a new team and also served as graphics for a critical group presentation.

creative ideas. Because visual mapping enables their ideas to remain visible once spoken, participants feel heard and honored.

Ideas flow freely because group members understand that critical thinking will have its due, and they will decide upon practical steps and roles when the time is right. Upon reflection, the group can address questions:

- **Purpose:** Did we remain on task?
- **Listening:** How well do we listen?
- **Equality:** Do we give equal time to everyone?
- **Interaction:** What is the nature of our interaction? Do we communicate clearly? Do we compete, cooperate, or support?

In this way, group members not only see the details of the content and issues they are evaluating, they are also able to understand the dynamics of their interactions. Then the group can discuss alternatives and make adjustments.

Graphic Facilitation

When one person is mapping, group members can watch the map and keep their attention focused on the discussion or presentation. If an idea comes up that relates to an earlier one, it can be recorded where it fits best. Thus, the final map is organized by category. Compare this to the lists of hastily written comments that often fill the walls of the room at the end of meetings.

Providing Process Feedback

Experienced mappers can also facilitate a discussion and provide feedback to the group. For example, key ideas and concerns that come up more than once can be emphasized on the map. Through "deep listening," the graphic facilitator can also note when the group makes assumptions. When someone says "Everyone knows . . ." or "It's a given that . . . ," the facilitator can map these comments and tag them with a certain color or symbol so that later the group can discuss these firmly held beliefs.

Once assumptions are open to conversation, the group can discover alternative ways of viewing the situation. Groups often believe they are stuck in an "either/or" situation. The choice seems black and white based upon the assumption that there are only two options and they must select one. When the graphic facilitator creates a space to creatively explore a range of "both/and" options, the group usually makes rapid progress.

Cycles

On other occasions, members of a group make statements that are important but are followed by silence, then a change of topic. These issues are probably the tough ones that often are ignored or left unspoken. The graphic facilitator may record them with a symbol that suggests they may be worth revisiting. As you may have guessed, this sort of feedback can make one unpopular unless the group has asked for

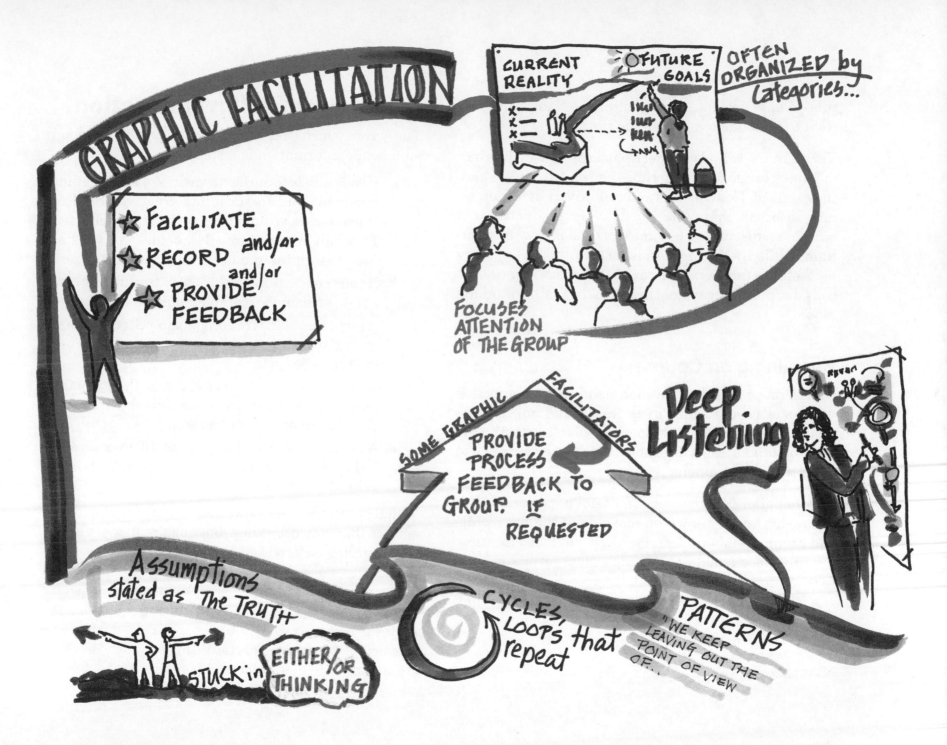

GRAPHIC FACILITATION

★ Facilitate
★ RECORD and/or
★ PROVIDE and/or
FEEDBACK

CURRENT REALITY — FUTURE GOALS — OFTEN ORGANIZED by Categories...

FOCUSES ATTENTION OF THE GROUP

SOME GRAPHIC FACILITATORS PROVIDE PROCESS FEEDBACK TO GROUP. IF REQUESTED

Deep Listening

Assumptions stated as The TRUTH

STUCK in EITHER/OR THINKING

CYCLES, LOOPS, that repeat

PATTERNS "WE KEEP LEAVING OUT THE POINT OF VIEW OF..."

this level of feedback and genuinely wants someone from the outside to observe the process.

Visual maps can also reflect patterns in which group members argue for a long time then end up back where they started. Noticing this and collectively determining how to break this cycle can be very productive. On occasion a discussion becomes focused on a very small item, while the big picture is lost. In this case it may be useful to take a break, review the visual maps, and consider the larger system in which the matter is taking place.

Remaining on Course

Often groups post their mission or values in conjunction with a strategic planning session. The graphic facilitator may ask, "How does this plan connect to the mission or values?" Often this leads the group back to their initial agreements.

Another approach that gives a useful perspective is for the facilitator to record on one side of the map while the group members describe their current situation. On the opposite side, the group's ideal future or goals for the next year are recorded. Between these two areas, the facilitator draws a valley or gap to focus discussion on how to create a bridge that will enable them to move across the gap.

Visual Form Follows Function

The way in which the group is mobilized often depends on how the information is displayed.

- If your aim is to surface a variety of ideas without judgment and to stimulate creativity and expansiveness, visual maps can be highly effective. They can inspire a free flow of ideas by working from the center and branching out.

- If your goal is to keep track of patterns over time, a flow, stream, or road map may be optimal.

- A large circular "cycle map" can reflect patterns and enable the group to explore how and where to break the cycle.

- If you feel you are at a crossroads, then a map of many directions may reveal alternative paths that you may have overlooked.

- As a creative exercise, you might even draw a hill or cloud obscuring a path, then ask, "What is behind this cloud?"

Visual processes are a powerful way of bringing to the surface that which we know, but don't realize we know! Once a group pattern is mapped, ripples extending from the pattern can encourage a group to explore the desired and unintended consequences. Other possibilities for creative maps include shooting stars firing from the pattern, roots growing into the ground, or sun-rays nurturing the central pattern. Images such as these often stimulate new ideas and insights.

Visual maps can take many forms. Design your map to reflect your topic. Be creative!

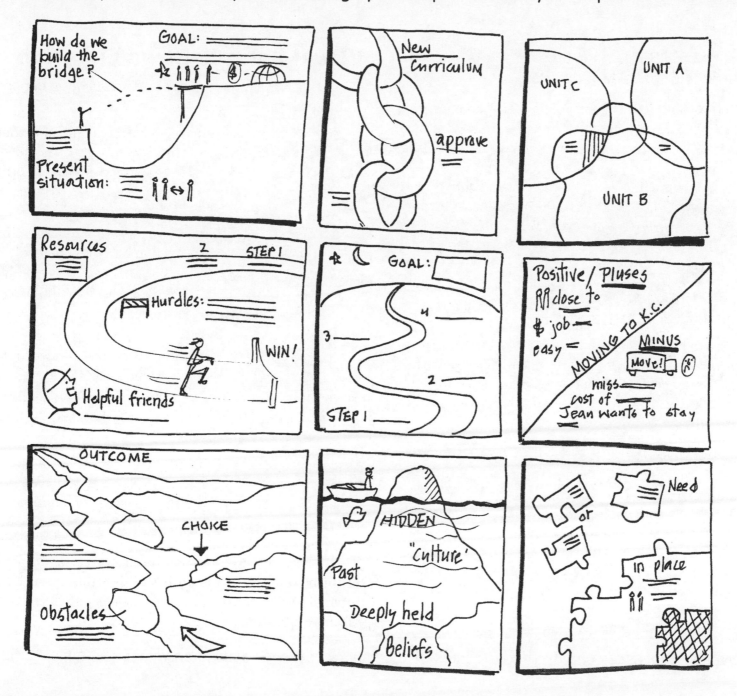

This overview map expresses one of the outcomes of a company retreat focused on values and aims.

Mapping Inner Space ©2002 Zephyr Press, Tucson, Arizona • 800-232-2187 • www.zephyrpress.com

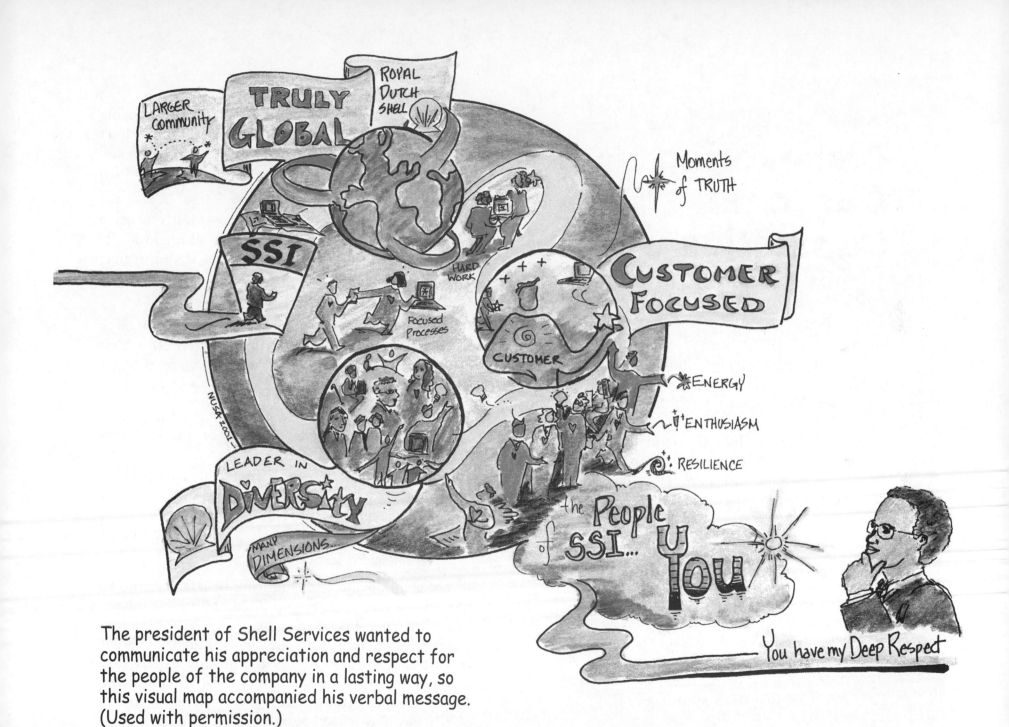

The president of Shell Services wanted to communicate his appreciation and respect for the people of the company in a lasting way, so this visual map accompanied his verbal message. (Used with permission.)

Chapter 7
Discovering Our Inner Capacities

Albert Einstein once said: "The words of the language, as they are written or spoken, do not seem to play any role in my mechanism of thought. The physical entities which seem to serve as elements in thought are certain signs and more or less clear images which can be voluntarily reproduced and combined. The above mentioned elements are, in my case, of visual and some of muscular type" (Root-Bernstein and Root-Bernstein 1999, 3).

Knowing and Sensing

Sparks of Genius: The Thirteen Thinking Tools of the World's Most Creative People takes a deep and broad view of great thinkers throughout history. The authors state, "Creative thinking and expression in every discipline are born of intuition and emotion. (Root-Bernstein and Root-Bernstein 1999, 6).

Our own limiting beliefs often pose a barrier to using our intuition and imagination fully. Most of us don't want to put too much faith in our intuitive senses and have trouble accepting credit when our hunches turn out to be accurate.

Aldous Huxley wrote that cognitive and receptive intuitive powers can be developed: "Both kinds of training are absolutely indispensable. If you neglect either of them, you'll never grow into a fully human being" (Huxley 1962, 255).

How can we foster intuition in children as well as in ourselves? In order to look at that question, let us first define some of the aspects of the intuitive process.

Intuitive experiences
- usually occur when we are in relaxed situations and not "working at" anything or trying to solve a problem
- occur spontaneously, seemingly out of the blue
- are frequently symbolic or kinesthetic in nature and can't be easily expressed in words
- often involve making new connections at an unconscious level

In order to move beyond limiting beliefs, assume for now that we all possess unlimited abilities to tap our inner knowing. Intuition takes many forms: We may hear an inner voice or imagine something that we can see with our eyes closed. Most of us have experienced a physical sensation that may be a warning that someone or something is approaching. We may not be able to say how we knew, but we did.

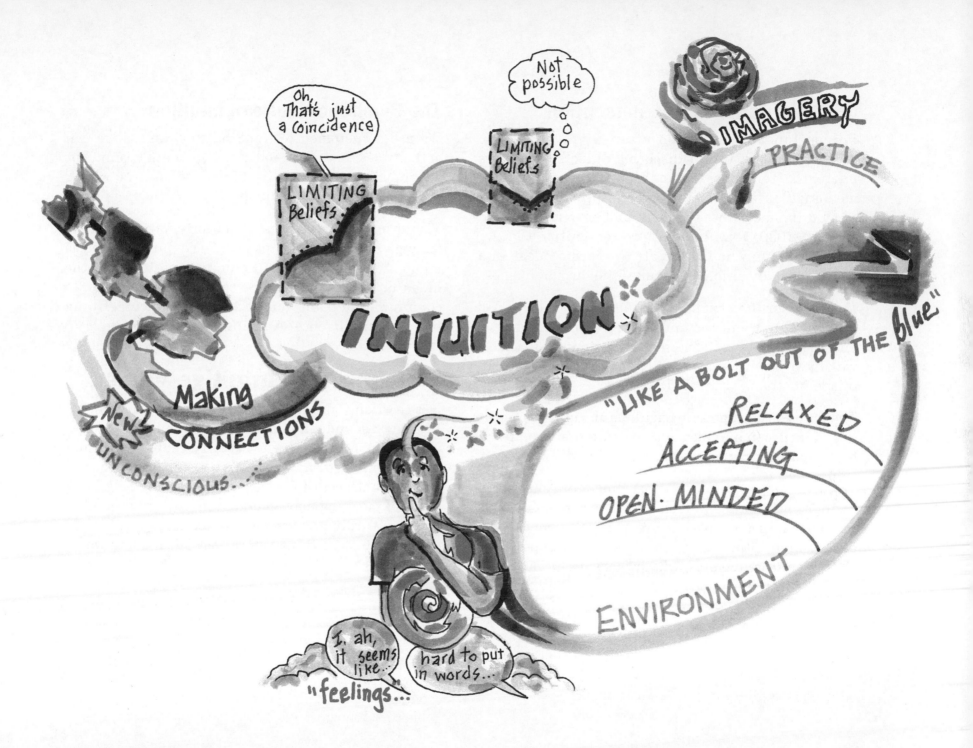

Intuition, Patterns, and Perception

Perception and intuition often involve pattern recognition. "Intuition discerns, detects, discovers patterns, forms relationships, properties, and meanings. Intuition helps you see through the facts, around the facts, into the facts, and beyond the facts" (Barrett 1989, 1–2). It is pattern recognition that we are developing when we create a record of ideas in a visual form. Intuition often takes the form of images.

"And now for the next step in examining intuition. We can now talk about the mind's eye, a common phrase, and an important one for creativity and innovation . . . we can work with images, we can image things, we can image-ine them" (Barrett 1989, 1–2).

The maps on the opposite page summarize the properties of intuition and also demonstrate that a map can be composed mostly of words.

To focus on our inner images and train ourselves further in the skill of imagination, we can make maps that have no set agenda and are purely the wanderings of the mind. Start with a large sheet of paper, play relaxing music, and draw whatever comes to you. Begin with a question, if you want, and see what answers appear. Or begin with an image and just doodle your way into the language of your intuitive knowing.

The Symbolic Nature of Intuition

We are accustomed to thinking that unless we can verbally describe or see something, it doesn't count, but our inner knowing may be difficult to put into words, yet it is very real and valuable.

Visual mapping provides a tool for expressing these feelings and sensory impulses. Once our intuition is mapped, we are closer to finding a way to refine the ideas or make them more concrete and easier to communicate. Can you actually practice refining intuitive intelligence? Noticing it is the first step.

Mapping Your Intuitive Voice

Notice when your intuition tends to be a bodily feeling, a voice or sound, an image, or a combination. At first you might note that you perceive feelings without corresponding meaning. If so, you can map lines or shapes that seem to correspond to these feelings. A sense of meaning may emerge from this process. If so, listen inwardly and wait for the possible meaning to emerge into something you can jot down using words or pictures.

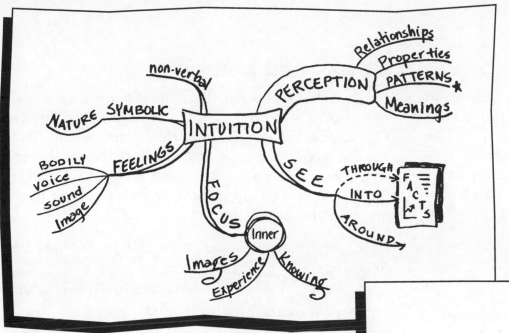

As you become more comfortable with drawing, allow yourself the freedom to draw, use shapes, and create symbols.

A word map, such as the one above, may be an easy place to begin. Add color or symbols if you wish.

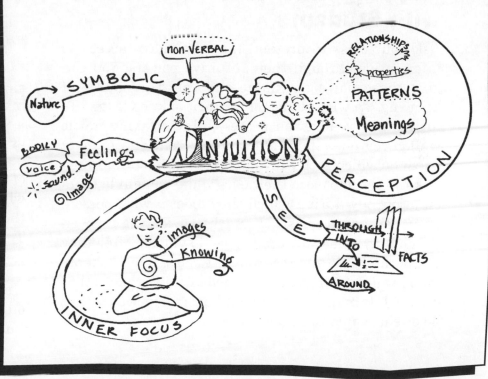

Go to the Roots

Our attitudes about intuition, expressing feelings in public, or admitting when we don't know the answer are beliefs that come from the culture around us. One way to move beyond limiting beliefs and assumptions is to trace the roots of your beliefs and then the "fruit" that results from these deeply held beliefs. This tree of assumptions may enable you to explore intuition and trust your feelings.

Mapping Inner Knowing with Students

Ask your class to pretend that they have access to information through their intuitive powers. You can give these powers a name such as "the source of knowing," "a wise guide," or "a spirit of knowledge." To further the realization process, play relaxing music while everyone sits comfortably in front of a piece of paper on which each will map his or her inner knowing. Ask the class to close their eyes while you guide them on a journey during which they meet a wise person. They can ask a question and listen for the answer, which may come in words or as a symbol. After they thank the guide and return to the classroom, students map in silence what they learned and other ideas that occur while mapping. If anyone had an experience that he or she wants to share, allow time for that.

Stress and Learning

It's clear that stress and threat limit our ability to use our cognitive processes fully. Psychologist Mihaly Csikszentmihalyi (pronounced chick-sent-me-high) has made a career investigating the factors that enable us to achieve a focused yet relaxed state of mind. He discovered that the opposite of stress is not lying back and watching television.

Csikszentmihalyi wanted to be able to answer the following:

- What makes our lives rewarding and meaningful?
- What contributes to creativity?
- How does motivation affect learning?

Flow and Learning

Csikszentmihalyi popularized the term "flow state" to describe the way we feel when we are actively and happily engaged in a challenging activity. These times of great fulfillment and richness of experience occur when there is a balance between our skill level and the degree of challenge involved in a task we enjoy. These are activities we want to be engaged in, with clear goals and immediate feedback.

Understanding how to create a flow state can enrich our lives and make learning more fun and appealing. Luckily, flow can occur during almost any activity.

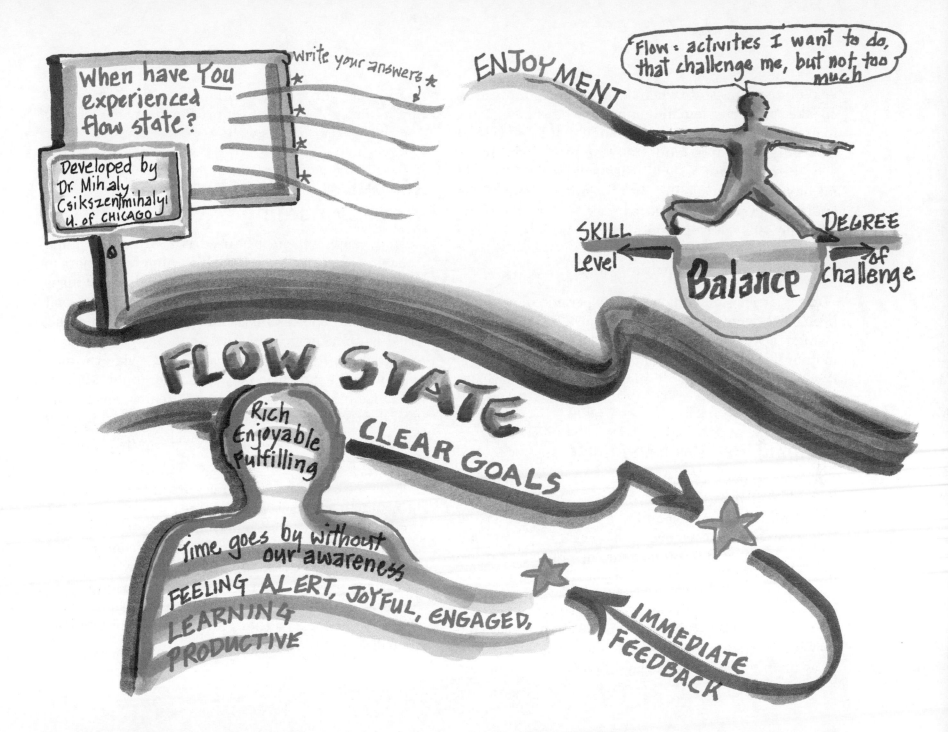

I experience flow state when listening to an interesting speaker or discussion and mapping what I hear. After mapping became easy for me, I found that I could stand in front of a large audience for hours, mapping everything I heard on large sheets of paper. I mapped all day, not even feeling hungry until the day was ending and I stopped to take a break. In those moments I had no sense of time and no self-consciousness. The inner voice I often hear judging my work was quiet. I guess she decided to go with the flow!

Writers, artists, and athletes also experience flow. When people are deeply focused, highly alert, feeling joy, and losing track of time, they are "in the flow." My grandmother felt that while gardening. My friend Ann feels it when she is dancing or engaged in improvisational theater.

Mapping the Flow Experience

The map on page 143 contains the key components of flow identified by Csikszentmihalyi. This map can be the beginning point for building a personal record of times you have experienced the flow state. Or you can use the same map to plan events or projects that are likely to produce a flow state for you, your students, or your employees.

As you explore this map, you might reflect on the role flow has played in your life. What circumstances tend to awaken a flow state? In addition to improving the quality of your experience, flow is a time when you are in a heightened state of productivity and actively engaged in learning as well.

Mapping in Coaching and Counseling

Visual mapping can also be used as a tool for individual coaching or counseling. While listening to the person you are coaching, you can record key events or ideas and show patterns with key words and symbols. Don't analyze your choices. Just follow your intuitive sense, trusting that there is an order that may become clear later. Ask questions for clarification and review the map with your client occasionally, asking for input. Maps of goals, feelings, relationships, even dreams, serve as an excellent record of sessions. People generally feel honored when their words and feelings are reflected in this manner.

You can also encourage your clients to create maps to bring to sessions as well. This same process can become a gift for a friend: Listen as your friend describes his or her life, goals, dreams, and concerns, then present your friend with a map that reflects whatever is important to him or her. This process is useful when one is at a crossroads. Map the options, then ask your friend to reflect on them and add his or her own thoughts over time.

Chapter 8

Anything Goes!

Alternatives to Mind Mapping

When I first learned to Mind Map, the rules served as important guidelines and made it easier for me to break from traditional note taking. For many purposes, such as daily planning, Mind Mapping that adheres to the basic rules works very well. However, I soon found myself moving away from the rules and creating maps that had no central image (gasp!), more than one word on a line, and other rebellious inventions. In fact I have remained intrigued with mapping by challenging myself to create visual representations that are new and designed to best represent the ideas I'm recording. These free-form maps are no longer technically Mind Maps, so let's call them *visual maps*.

When you feel ready to experiment by creating your personal style of mapping, you may want to consider these guidelines:

Diversity

Allow your maps to be as varied as possible. In this way you are continually challenging yourself to find new ways to put ideas on paper (or computers, place mats, or T-shirts). The intuitive, holistic processing of your brain will remain more engaged if the process doesn't become too routine. Even your daily plan maps can look different every time you make one.

Anything Goes

Try making a map that is mural size and takes up an entire wall, or one that has little paper doors with messages behind them, or one written within segments of a geodesic dome. How about mapping evaluations or invitations to a party? No limits!

Start Anywhere

Begin your map wherever you wish.

- Make a giant image on the page and fill it in with your notes, ideas, and symbols.
- Record two ideas, one on each half of the paper, and compare or contrast them across the page.
- Make the map resemble an actual road map, a jigsaw puzzle, or a giant game board.

The illustration on the following page suggests several other configurations that you may find useful.

These maps encourage action planning using ideas from a presentation. They illustrate alternative configurations for Mind Maps.

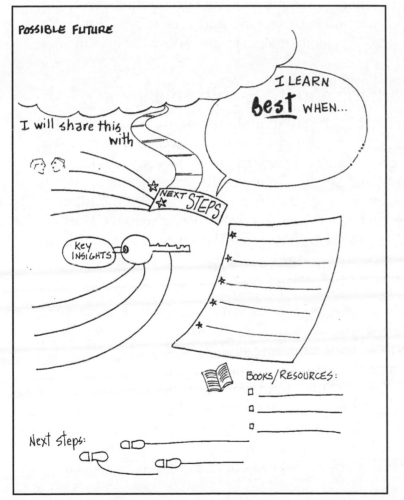

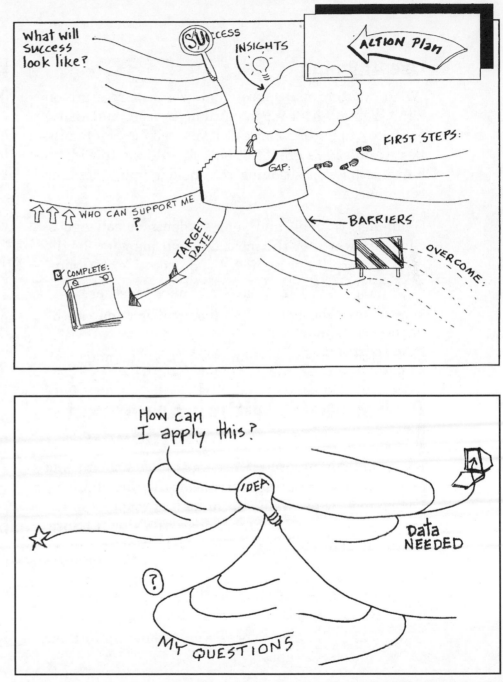

Use Anything

When creating maps, use whatever resources are on hand. You might want to cut images from magazines or photographs for a map about yourself for your family. Post-it notes are great not only for adding new ideas, but also for repositioning to consider many possible combinations.

Challenge yourself and your students or colleagues. Give an award for the most unusual maps or for the most unique idea presented. Ask provocative questions:

- Is it possible to weave two maps together?
- Can several people work on one long map at the same time?
- How can we use computers for visual maps?

A View from Within: Advanced Mapping Project for Students

For a challenging project, assign students the task of creating a visual map about someone they are studying. For example, what would the inner landscape, or mindscape, of Benjamin Franklin, Leonardo da Vinci, Cochise, Abraham Lincoln, Eleanor Roosevelt, Martin Luther King, Marie Antoinette, or George W. Bush look like?

- What would be emphasized?
- What connections between ideas might be made?
- Which life experiences would show up in their inner landscapes?

Multiple Intelligence Theory and Mapping

As many educators know, Dr. Howard Gardner developed a theory of multiple intelligences. To the usual math and verbal skills, he added interpersonal (relationships with others), intrapersonal (understanding ourselves), bodily/kinesthetic, visual, and musical/rhythmic. Recently, he added an eighth: the naturalist intelligence.

Patterns and the Eighth Intelligence

In practice the eight intelligences are not separate but integrated in unique combinations as one complex, ever-changing intelligence that is woven with the mind, body, and spirit. The naturalist intelligence relates to the capacity to identify plant species and the talent to assign them to new or established taxonomy (Gardner 2000). To me Gardner's definition suggests the ability to recognize patterns and notice the relationship of parts to the whole.

When students seek patterns in the world around them, they see order within chaos, which builds confidence in their understanding of how the world works. Robert Barkman points out that pattern recognition isn't limited to nature and the naturalist intelligence. There are patterns in numbers, musical scores, and the way we think and interact (Barkman 1999). It seems likely that Gardner's eighth intelligence not only has its own identity but also is used to enrich the other seven.

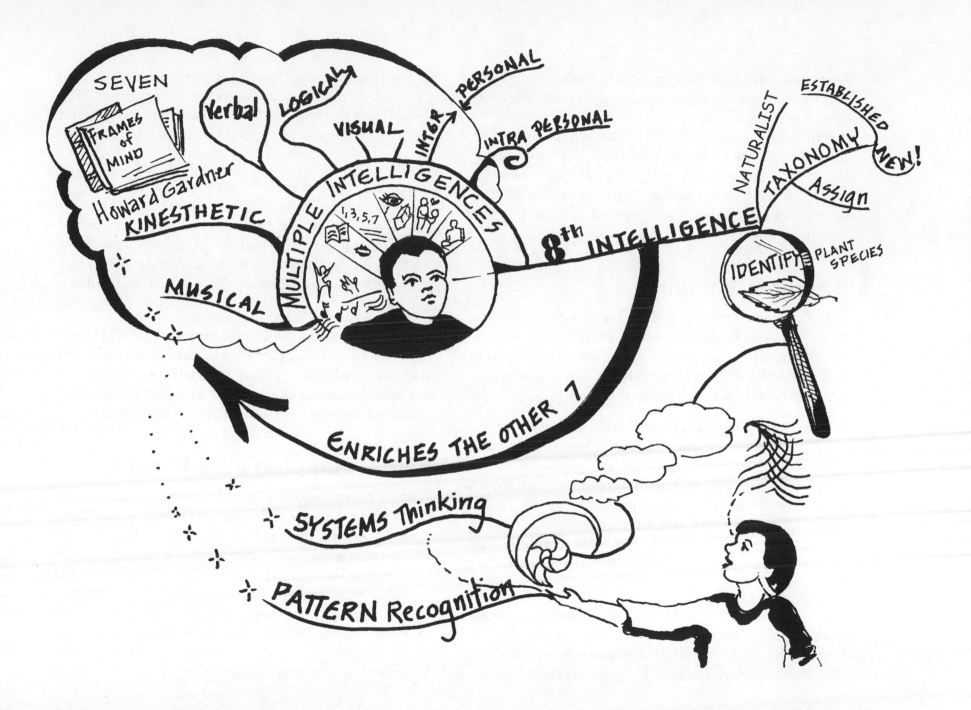

Our traditional system of recording ideas is linear and presupposes a simple pattern of left to right (this only varies a bit in other countries where it may be up to down, right to left, but still a linear pattern). When mapping, we are given the exciting opportunity to use the composition of the map, the ability to add new ideas where they fit, and the possibility of coding similar aspects by color or with symbols, all according to our own unique sense of patterns.

Systems Thinking

Mapping relationships and patterns leads us to the ability to record an entire system, such as a work team, classroom, school, or method of education. Each system is contained within a larger one, so we might map a small system or a vast and complex one.

Within any system there are interactions and actions that create outcomes. One of the values of looking at a system is to study the possible consequences of our actions. We can also see how one small event might set off a chain reaction. In business settings, the act of discussing the system and attempting to map it often brings people much closer to shared understandings, or surfaces areas that need to be considered before taking any action.

The symbols and style for mapping complex systems developed by Daniel Kim and his colleagues are extremely valuable, especially in complex business settings. (For more information, see Pegasus Communications in the Resources section.) The maps on the opposite page were created while working with author Meg Wheatley. The systems she focuses on are those found in nature, which can be applied to human organizations.

When studying the natural system depicted in the map on the left, you can see how these principles could apply to a healthy organization. The map on the right uses the principle of a core identity, necessary for all living things, and applies it to the shared identity or "self" of an organization. From that central identity spin our basic assumptions, sense of purpose, values, and activities.

On page 153, a map made while working with systems theorist Fritjof Capra reflects the relationship of systems *within* systems in biology. These can inform our thinking about the systems in which we live and work and the larger systems that contain them.

Visual Mapping as a Career

When I began mapping meetings and conferences, I didn't know of anyone else engaged in such work. Then I met Nusa and we began to share ideas about how to create maps in real time, during meetings. In California, David Sibbet and his colleagues were independently developing The Grove Consultants, which emphasizes storyboards, process maps, and information-charting on large wall-sheets of paper for group processes. See The Grove Consultants in the Resources for information about their programs as well

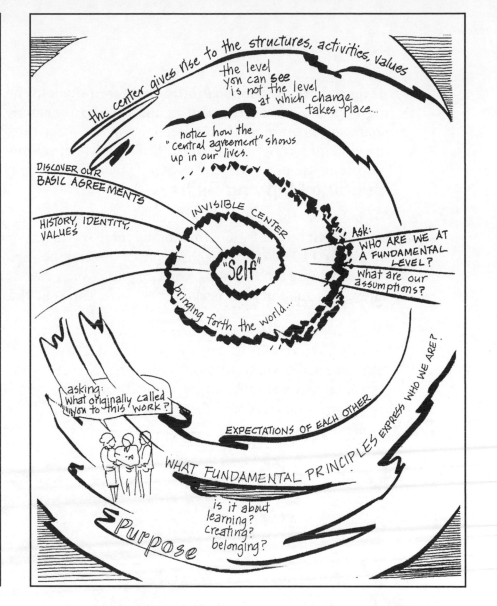

The above map represents living systems and their web of relationships. The use of curving lines alone suggests the natural world. This map reflects Meg Wheatley's presentation at one of the annual Systems Thinking in Action conferences, sponsored by Pegasus Communications.

The spiraling movement of lines on this map emphasizes that any living system continuously recreates itself from its core identity. This sense of self is the way we bring forth our world—as individuals and as organizations.

as for a company that specializes in recording maps in digital format, and a national organization that sponsors conferences for visual recorders.

Building Mapping Skills

To practice real-time visual recording, listen to an audiotaped presentation. In a comfortable setting, map on either 11" x 17" or flip-chart paper. Audiotapes are great training tools because you can pause and rewind, allowing time for your practice sessions. Tapes at the library or from New Dimensions Radio (see Resources) allow you to learn about something new and interesting while developing advanced mapping skills.

The best way to become a skilled visual mapper is to practice. Teaching mapping to others will anchor the learning. Introduce mapping to colleagues, a group of students, or family members you think will enjoy this process. Your own capacity to make connections and think creatively will increase, as will your ability to see and record the systems within systems that make up our world.

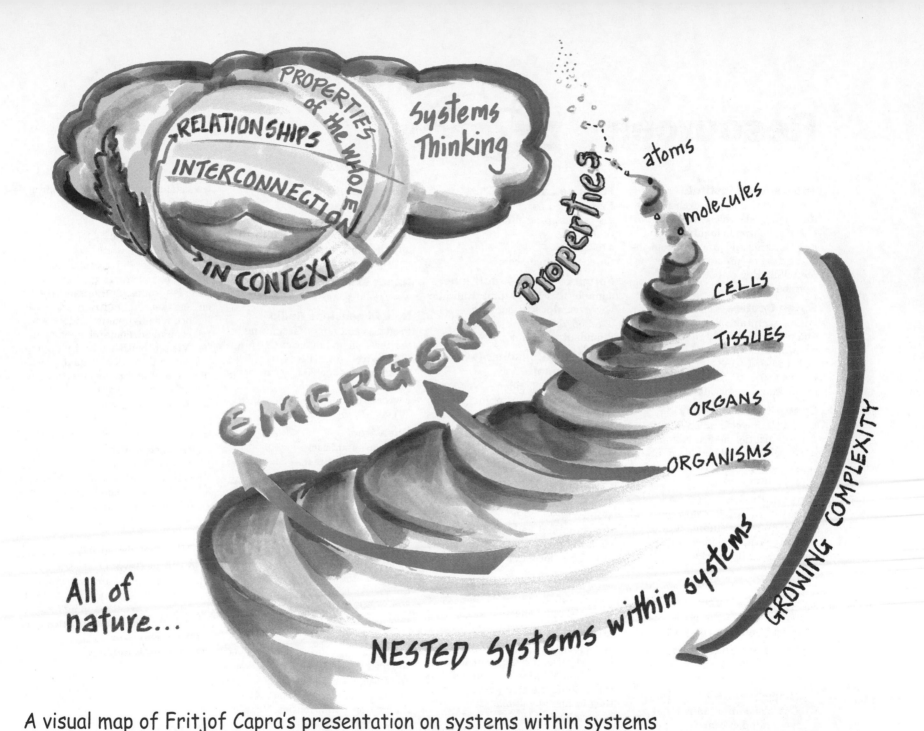

A visual map of Fritjof Capra's presentation on systems within systems

Resources

The Berkana Institute
Educational and research foundation that seeks to create communities of support and inquiry to explore new thinking and practice about the organizing of human endeavor.
Meg Wheatley, cofounder
www.berkana.org

Buzan Centres
Offers training in Mind Mapping and other Buzan techniques.
www.mind-map.com
U.S.: 561-881-0188
U.K.: 44-(0)1202-674676
buzan@mind-map.com

Center for Ecoliteracy
Fritjof Capra, cofounder
An organization dedicated to fostering experience and understanding of the natural world.
www.ecoliteracy.org

Chrysanthemum Design
Chrisann Brennan makes pre- and post-conference summary murals and large balancing mandalas.
www.chrysanthemum.com
650-854-9863
Chrisann@differnet.com

Computer Software
Free trial versions of programs for creating Mind Maps on your PC:

Inspiration Software, Inc.:
Download Inspiration at www.inspiration.com

Mindjet:
Download MindManager at www.mindjet.com

Florence Landau, M.A.
Experienced psychologist who uses visual mapping for coaching and counseling.
415-383-3654
florence@hotmail.com

Forum of Visual Practitioners
Jennifer Landau, graphic facilitator
www.visualpractitioner.org
415-255-2893
jhlandau@earthlink.net

The Grove Consultants International
David Sibbet, founder
Consults with teams, organizations, and communities using graphic recording and facilitation. Provides training for graphic recorders.
www.grove.com
800-49-GROVE

Landau Chartworks
Jessica and Julien Landau, digital archivists
Captures and color-corrects large visual maps into digital images of any size or format, available in any format.
www.landauchartworks.com
415-435-4973
jessica@landauchartworks.com

LifePlays
Workshops designed to enhance the joy and power of being in an authentic relationship with yourself and others. Includes improvisational theater and visual mapping.
Anne: 650-712-1603

The Mozart Effect Resource Center
Don Campbell, founder
Information about Campbell's work and the use of music for learning.
www.mozarteffect.com

Nancy Margulies
www.mind-scapes.net

New Dimensions Radio
Produces and offers fascinating interviews (on audiotape or CD) originally aired on NPR. Interviews make excellent subjects for mapping practice.
www.newdimensions.org
707-468-5215

Nusa Maal
www.nusamaal.com
(See also SenseSmart.)

Pegasus Communications, Inc.
Daniel Kim, cofounder
Supports a community of systems-thinking practitioners through *The Systems Thinker* newsletter, books, audio- and videotapes, the annual Systems Thinking in Action conference and other events.
www.pegasuscom.com
800-272-0945
info@pegasuscom.com

Robert E. Horn
Visiting scholar at Stanford University (Program on People, Computers, and Design; Center for the Study of Language and Information), Horn is the creator of Information Mapping and Hypertext.

www.stanford.edu/~rhorn/index.html
415-775-7377
hornbob@earthlink.net

SenseSmart, Inc.
Nusa Maal, founder
Provides interactive consulting, facilitation, and training to help individuals, groups, and organizations engage their full multisensory intelligence for alignment, understanding, communication, and productivity. For Visual Synthesis and mapping resources, links, downloadable templates, and other continuations to *Mapping Inner Space:*
www.sensesmart.com
301-652-8464
SenseSmart@aol.com

Take Action! Inc.
Dana Wright, founder
Consults with organizations, teams, and individuals, using visual tools such as graphic charts.
www.take-action.com
408-866-2575
dwright@take-action.com

The World Café
The World Café is a process for encouraging the emergence of shared intelligence. Visual mapping records insights that emerge from café-style conversations.
www.theworldcafe.com

Bibliography

Arnheim, R. 1983. *Art and Visual Perception: A Psychology of the Creative Eye.* 2d ed. Berkeley: University of California Press.

Barkman, R. 1999. *Science through Multiple Intelligences: Patterns That Inspire Inquiry.* Tucson, Ariz.: Zephyr Press.

Barrett, D. 1989. "Intuition and Creative Thinking." *The Human Intelligence Newsletter.* (February–March).

Brewer, C., and D. Campbell. 1991. *Rhythms of Learning: Creative Tools for Developing Lifelong Skills.* Tucson, Ariz.: Zephyr Press.

Brookes, M. 1986. *Drawing with Children: A Creative Method for Adult Beginners, Too.* Los Angeles: J. P. Tarcher.

Buzan, T. 1996. *The Mind Map Book: How to Use Radiant Thinking to Maximize Your Brain's Untapped Potential.* Reprint ed. New York: Plume.

Cameron, J. 1992. *The Artist's Way: A Spiritual Path to Higher Creativity.* New York: J. P. Tarcher/Putnam Books.

Campbell, B. 1994. *The Multiple Intelligences Handbook: Lesson Plans and More.* Stanwood, Wash.: Campbell and Assoc.

Campbell, D. 2000. *The Mozart Effect for Children: Awakening Your Child's Mind, Health, and Creativity with Music.* New York: William Morrow and Co.

Cousins, N. 1989. *Head First: The Biology of Hope.* New York: E. P. Dutton.

Covey, S. R. 1990. *The Seven Habits of Highly Effective People.* New York: Fireside.

Csikszentmihalyi, M. 1990. *Flow: The Psychology of the Optimal Experience.* New York: Harper & Row.

De Bono, E. 1990. *Lateral Thinking: Creativity Step-by-Step.* Reissue ed. New York: Harper & Row.

Dvorak, R. R.1993. *The Magic of Drawing.* Montara, Calif.: Inkwell Press.

Frutiger, A. 1998. *Signs and Symbols: Their Design and Meaning.* New York: Watson-Guptill Publications.

Gardner, H. 1983. *Frames of Mind.* New York: Harper & Row.

———.1993. *Creating Minds: An Anatomy of Creativity Seen Through the Lives of Freud, Einstein, Picasso, Stravinsky, Eliot, Graham, and Gandhi.* New York: Basic Books.

———. 2000. *Intelligence Reframed: Multiple Intelligences for the 21st Century.* New York: Basic Books.

Gilbert, A. 2001. *Braindemonium.* Tucson, Ariz.: Zephyr Press. [posters]

Goleman, D. 1997. *Emotional Intelligence.* New York: Bantam.

Gross, R. 1988. *Peak Learning.* Los Angeles: Audio Renaissance Tapes, Inc. [audiocassette]

Horn, R. 1999. *Visual Language: Global Communication for the 21st Century.* Bainbridge Island, Wash.: MacroVU, Inc.

Huxley, A. 1962. *Island.* New York: Harper and Row.

Kaufeldt, M. 1999. *Begin with the Brain: Orchestrating the Learner-Centered Classroom.* Tucson, Ariz.: Zephyr Press.

Kline, P. 1988. *The Everyday Genius.* Arlington, Va.: Great Ocean Publishers.

Kunzler, D. 1998. *Brain Smart.* Tucson, Ariz.: Zephyr Press. [posters]

Lazear, D. 2000. *Pathways of Learning: Teaching Students and Parents about Multiple Intelligences.* Tucson, Ariz.: Zephyr Press.

LeDoux, Joseph. 1998. *The Emotional Brain: The Mysterious Underpinnings of Emotional Life.* New York: Touchstone.

Margulies, N. 1991. *Yes, You Can Draw!* Aylesbury, Bucks, UK: Accelerated Learning Systems.

———. 1993. *Maps, Mindscapes, and More.* Tucson, Ariz.: Zephyr Press. [video]

———. 1995. *Map It!: Tools for Charting the Vast Territories of Your Mind.* Tucson, Ariz.: Zephyr Press. [comic book]

———. 1996. *Inside Brian's Brain.* Tucson, Ariz.: Zephyr Press.

Margulies, N., and M. Gelb. 1989. *The Mind Map.* Washington, D.C.: High Performance Learning.

Margulies, N., and R. Sylwester. 1998a. *Emotion and Attention.* Discover Your Brain series. Tucson, Ariz.: Zephyr Press.

———. 1998b. *Memory.* Discover Your Brain series. Tucson, Ariz.: Zephyr Press.

McCloud, S. 2000. *Reinventing Comics.* New York: HarperCollins Publishers, Inc.

Nicolaides, K. 1990. *The Natural Way to Draw: A Working Plan for Art Study.* Boston, Mass.: Houghton Mifflin.

Palmer, P. 1993. *To Know As We Are Known: Education as a Spiritual Journey.* Reprint Edition. San Francisco: Harper and Row.

———. 1997. *The Courage to Teach: Exploring the Inner Landscape of a Teacher's Life.* San Francisco: Jossey-Bass.

Root-Bernstein, R., and M. Root-Bernstein. 1999. *Sparks of Genius: The Thirteen Thinking Tools of the World's Most Creative People.* Boston, Mass.: Houghton Mifflin.

Senge, P. 2000. *Schools That Learn: A Fifth Discipline Fieldbook for Educators, Parents, and Everyone Who Cares about Education.* New York: Doubleday.

Sonneman, M. R. 1997. *Beyond Words: A Guide to Drawing Out Ideas.* Berkeley, Calif.: Ten Speed Press.

Sylwester, R. 1998. "The Down-Shifting Dilemma." Unpublished paper.

Wenger, W. 1990. *Toward a General Theory of Creativity and Genius.* Aurora, N.Y.: United Educational Services.

Wheatley, M. 1999. *Leadership and the New Science: Discovering Order in a Chaotic World.* San Francisco: Berrett-Koehler Publishers, Inc.

Wheatley, M., and M. Kellner-Rogers. 1996. *A Simpler Way.* San Francisco: Berrett-Koehler Publishers, Inc.

About the Authors

LEARNING

MINDFULNESS
QI GONG
SLOWING DOWN, sort of...

COMICS, BOOKS, VIDEOS
next... a novel
AUTHOR

The World Café
Planning Hosting

MINDSCAPES

I look for the way things will turn

for the form things want to unfold

to any shape that may be summoning me...

Coach
Teacher
Mentor
Artist

Nancy Margulies, MA.
www.mind·scapes.net

Multi-sensory Intelligence
Diversity
Relationships
Self awareness

Access
Original
Full potential

Workshops

BELIEVERS IN INFINITE Possibilities

VISUAL SYNTHESIS® Presenter.
Teacher
Facilitator

BADLANDS

Co·author·
COACH
Artist

Nusa Maal   www.sensesmart.com

Index